Food and Gender

Food in History and Culture

A series edited by *Carole M. Counihan*, Dept. of Anthropology, Millersville University, Millersville, Pennsylvania and *Steven L. Kaplan*, Dept. of History, Cornell University, Ithaca, New York

Food in History and Culture examines the history of food, food consumption and food-based rituals in order to provide a greater understanding of culture and society.

Volume 1
Food and Gender: Identity and Power
Edited by Carole M. Counihan and Steven L. Kaplan

This book is part of a series. The publisher will accept continuation orders which may be cancelled at any time and which provide for automatic billing and shipping of each title in the series upon publication. Please write for details.

Food and Gender

Identity and Power

Edited by

Carole M. Counihan

Millersville University
Millersville, Pennsylvania, USA

and

Steven L. Kaplan

Cornell University
Ithaca, New York, USA

harwood academic publishers

Australia Canada China France Germany India
Japan Luxembourg Malaysia The Netherlands Russia
Singapore Switzerland Thailand

Amsteldijk 166
1st Floor
1079 LH Amsterdam
The Netherlands

Some of the chapters in this book were originally published in either volume 1 or volume 3 of the journal *Food and Foodways*.

Front cover: *BAMBOLINA, PANE PER BAMBINI* (Doll Bread for Children), Dualchi, Sardinia. Reprinted with permission of the University of Cagliari, Italy.
Copyright © 1973 University of Cagliari, Italy.

British Library Cataloguing in Publication Data

Food and gender : identity and power. – (Food in history and culture ; v. 1)
   1. Food – Social aspects 2. Food – Symbolic aspects 3. Food – Symbolic aspects – Sex differences 4. Nutrition – Sex differences
   I. Counihan, Carole M.   II. Kaplan, Steven L.
   363.8

ISBN   90-5702-568-X

CONTENTS

INTRODUCTION TO THE SERIES

Food in History and Culture seeks to examine and illuminate the role of food in various cultures and throughout history, in order to provide a greater understanding of civilization and society. Food contributes to the creation of people's lives—socially, economically, politically, morally and nutritionally—in powerful but often subtle ways. This series explores the history of food production, distribution and consumption, as well as the role of food in rituals. In their analyses, the authors included in *Food in History and Culture* are committed to the idea of food as a matter of social, as much as biological, importance.

Carole Counihan
Steve Kaplan

ACKNOWLEDGMENTS

We thank Millersville and Cornell Universities for supporting our work. We are grateful to our editor Monica Glina for performing miracles to bring this book to fruition. Finally, we are indebted to Millersville anthropology major Angela Reisinger for preparing the index.

"FOOD AND GENDER: IDENTITY AND POWER"

Carole M. Counihan

INTRODUCTION

The value of studying food as a path to understanding culture and history has by now been well established. The pioneering work of anthropologist Audrey Richards (1932, 1939) in the early part of this century launched the formal acknowledgment of foodways as an effective prism through which to illuminate human life. Since then, a growing number of studies in the social sciences and humanities have contributed depth and breadth to the study of food and culture. A decade of publishing the journal *Food and Foodways* has firmly established the myriad interdisciplinary contributions made by the study of human alimentation.

Food and Gender: Identity and Power marks the first in a series of planned collections anthologizing articles originally published in *Food and Foodways*. We chose the focus of our first volume because of the clear significance of food-centered activities and meanings to the constitution of gender relations and identities across cultures. Gender matters in food centered activities as it does in "structuring human societies, their histories, ideologies, economic systems and political structures" (Moore 1988: 6). We highlight two central questions about food and gender in this volume: (1) How does control of food production, distribution and consumption contribute to men's and women's power and social position? (2) How does food symbolically connote maleness and femaleness and establish the social value of men and women?

FOOD, POWER, AND GENDER

We focus on power and foodways in two principal ways. First, there is the power that society allocates or denies to men and women through their

1

access to and control of one essential resource: food. Men's and women's ability to produce, provide, distribute and consume food is a key measure of their power. This ability varies according to their culture, their class, and their family organization, and the overall economic structure of their society.

The second meaning of power we examine is personal power: whether men's and women's relationship to food and its meanings contributes to a valued sense of self. Men's and women's attitudes about their bodies, the legitimacy of their appetites, and the importance of their food work reveal whether their self-concept is validating or denigrating. We are concerned with how their relationship to food may facilitate gender complementarity and mutual respect or produce gender hierarchy.

FOOD AND POWER: PRODUCTION, DISTRIBUTION AND CONSUMPTION

There are many important studies that link the control of food to political and economic power. In his comprehensive historical study *Famine*, Arnold (1988: 3) claims that "food was, and continues to be, power in a most basic, tangible and inescapable form." Lappé and Collins (1986) argue that hunger is the clearest sign of powerlessness, for hunger means one lacks the control to satisfy one's most basic subsistence need. Many authors point out that women very often suffer hunger and famine more severely than men because of their socio-economic and political subordination in many countries of the world (e.g. Arnold 1988; Lappé and Collins 1986; Leghorn and Roodkowsky 1977; Vaughn 1987).

Class, caste, race and gender hierarchies are maintained, in part, through differential control over and access to food (Goody 1982). Different consumption patterns are one of the ways the rich distinguish themselves from the poor and men from women (Bennett 1943; Fitchen 1988; Mintz 1985; Weismantel 1988). Many studies demonstrate that men eat first, best, and most. According to Adams (1990: 189), "The message of male dominance is conveyed through meat eating—both in its symbolism and in its reality." In *Sweetness and Power*, Mintz (1985) describes at length how control of sugar production and consumption contributed to class hierarchy and colonial dominance but neglects consideration of gender. However, a telling photograph conveys the unstated message of assumed male control. The caption reads "Etienne Tholoniat, a great French sugar baker, puts the finishing touches on a life-size chocolate nude with spun-sugar hair. She is lying on a bed of six hundred sugar roses" (Mintz 1985: 184). Here the active, powerful male literally defines the female as a supine, passive, object of consumption—a food symbol for cultural practice mirroring male–female power relations.

In this volume, both Kahn and Pollock demonstrate how gender is constituted through men's and women's roles in the production, distribution and symbolism of food. Kahn shows that for the Wamirans of Papua New Guinea, men and women establish their complementarity and balance through their roles in the production of taro, the most important food both symbolically and nutritionally. Yet taro is the quintessentially masculine food; it "is alone capable of symbolically communicating male status and virility." Taro plants are men's "children," and they metaphorically enable men to balance women's creation of human children. Taro stands for masculinity and is the most important food distributed at the political feasts where men jockey for power in the village. Yet women's essential contributions to taro production reinforce their needed role in Wamiran economy and culture, just as men's recognized role in reproducing children reinforces their importance. By making a symbolic parallel between taro and children, and involving men and women in the production of both, Wamirans equalize male and female powers (see also Kahn 1986).

In this volume, Pollock shows that among the Culina of the western Amazon, men and women similarly establish their distinctive identities as well as their social and economic interdependence through the production and distribution of food. A clear sexual division of labor allocates most of the gardening to women and the hunting to men. The sexes are identified with the different products of their labor: women with vegetables and men with meat. Marriage involves the reciprocal exchange of "food for food: meat for cultivated garden products." In this egalitarian culture, male and female differential control over diverse aspects of the food system is explicitly balanced in belief and practice.

In many cultures, the exchange of food is a most profound way of making social connection. Mauss (1967) has shown the pervasive cultural power of the gift which keeps individuals constantly indebted to each other and continuously engaged in positive interaction through giving. Food is an extremely important component of reciprocal exchanges, more so than any other object or substance. As Sahlins (1972: 215) says: "By comparison with other stuff, food is more readily, or more necessarily shared."

Because of this, food is often a medium of exchange, connection, and distinction between men and women, as noted for the Culina above. However, exchanges must be reciprocal to maintain equality. McIntosh and Zey in this volume point out the lack of reciprocity in men's and women's food exchanges in the United States. They explore Lewin's (1943) concept of women as "gatekeepers" of food into the home, which implies that women hold much power over food distribution. They suggest that while women may have responsibility over provisioning food, "responsibility is not equivalent of control" which may in fact reside with men. Their work contributes to that of DeVault (1990) and Charles and Kerr (1989) who also recognize women's widespread responsibility for food provisioning in both the United States and England. These authors see women's food provisioning as a mixed bag, one that is a potential source of influence on husbands and children through the ability to give them a valued substance—food—but one that also is linked with female subordination through women's need to serve, satisfy, and defer to others, particularly husbands or boyfriends.

In U.S. society, female college students report that they feel ashamed to eat in front of men with whom they have a romantic involvement, so they may offer food but not eat it (Counihan 1992). They also report that men denigrate and gain power over them by saying they eat too much or are too fat (Millman 1980; Counihan 1992). In gender stratified cultures as diverse as England (Charles and Kerr 1988), Italy (Counihan 1988), Mexico (Friedlander 1979), and Andean Ecuador (Weismantel 1988), men exert control over women by claiming the authority to judge the meal cooked by them, but women do not usually have a similar power because men rarely cook, and when they do so claim commendation simply for taking on this task (DeVault 1990).

The power relations around food mirror the power of the sexes in general. Whereas men's economic status is demonstrated by their control of food purchasing (Charles and Kerr 1988), women wield considerable power in all cultures by their control of meal planning and cooking. Behar (1989) discusses how women in 18th century Mexico fed ensorseled food to husbands to tame their abusive behavior. Adams (1990) argues that patriarchal power in Western society is embodied in the practice of eating meat which, she argues, involves the linked objectification and subordination of animals and women. But women can rebel through vegetarianism which, from this perspective, is a political statement: a rejection of patriarchal power and values, an expression of feminism, and a claiming of female power over self and nature. Among the Zumbaguan Indians of Andean Ecuador (Weismantel 1988: 28–29), the senior female is in charge of preparing and serving meals. This gives her the ability to determine hierarchies by the order in which she serves people and the contents of the plate she gives them (Weismantel 1988: 182). A woman can even punish her errant husband when he finally returns from a drinking spree by serving him massive quantities of rich food which the husband, by force of etiquette, is obliged to eat with extremely unpleasant physical results.

GENDER, FOOD, AND THE SUPERNATURAL

In many cultures, food is instrumental in maintaining good relations between humans and their deities. Ancient Greeks, and many other peoples, use food sacrifices as a means of propitiating their gods (Détienne and Vernant 1989; Mauss 1967). In patriarchal cultures, men claim exclusive mediating powers with the supernatural; in more egalitarian cultures, women's control over food carries over into an essential mediating role in rituals supplicating gods and spirits. In Catholic ritual, for example, only male priests can perform the ritual of transubstantiation, where the bread and wine are converted into the body and blood of Christ. Interestingly, Medieval holy women sometimes subverted the totality of male control by refusing to eat anything but the consecrated host, challenging the legitimacy of some priests by vomiting the host and thus claiming it unconsecrated, and by exuding miraculous foods from their own bodies (Bell 1985; Bynum 1986).

In this volume, both March and Van Esterik show how women use food gifts in religious rituals to coerce supernatural beings to act favorably towards humans. March discusses Sherpa and Tamang Buddhists who live in the highlands of Nepal. Although distinctive peoples, they share many religious beliefs and rituals. Among both populations, hospitality, especially in the form of commensality, is central to maintaining relations between humans and gods (see also Ortner 1978). March points out that "women and symbols of femaleness are crucial at all levels of exchange" due to their central role in food, especially beer, production and their symbolic association "with the many blessings—of health, strength, fertility, prosperity, plenitude, and general increase—that fermented and distilled offerings are thought to secure." The essentially female cast of offerings to the gods underlines the ambiguous nature of all offerings: that they are simultaneously altruistic and selfish, simultaneously a gift and an effort to secure a return.

Van Esterik in this volume also underlines the significance of women's role in feeding and food gifts. Because women prepare and control food, they are agents for ritual and religious knowledge and food offerings. They underscore the "'connectedness' of the living and the dead" by preparing food for the ancestors and they give food to the Buddhist monks and deities central to their religious expression. The male/meat, female/vegetable association that obtains among groups as diverse as Amazon Indians (Pollock this volume, Siskind 1973) and Western urbanites (Adams 1990) is also symbolically significant. Women feel compelled to offer meat to monks because it is a highly valued food requiring economic sacrifice, but meat is also tainted because of the Buddhist prohibition on killing. "The contradiction between feminine generous giving of food to the monks and masculine ascetic rejection of such sensuous pleasures as eating lies at the heart of Buddhist belief and practice." Women constantly negotiate the contradiction by offering food to several monks; they know that some will reject meat to affirm their holiness and others will accept it to validate the women's sacrifice.

Just as giving food creates connection, refusing it severs connection. Both giving and refusing can be a means of attaining power. Kahn illustrates how Wamiran village chiefs demonstrate their power both by distributing food at feasts and by resisting its consumption through wielding powerful hunger suppression magic on themselves. The ability to dampen appetite is a valued skill in cultures where periodic food shortages may plague the population. Among Melanesian peoples, this appears to be a magic held exclusively by men, who are the main chiefs and religious practitioners (Young 1986). It generally is practiced to benefit all the population, however, not just men.

Counihan's two articles in this volume reflect on the fact that for over eight centuries, European and American women have refused food as a path to achievement and mastery in a world over which they have had few other means of control. Today, modern anorexics starve themselves, sometimes to death, to achieve physical and spiritual perfection. Their behavior is strikingly similar to that of medieval holy women in the fourteenth, fifteenth, and sixteenth centuries although the meanings of their behaviors are rather different because of the different cultural contexts in which they occur (Bell 1985; Bynum 1987; Brumberg 1988). Medieval holy women fasted for religious and spiritual perfection: holiness. They used eating or fasting as a path to reach God and to circumvent patriarchal familial, religious and civil authority. Some women achieved sainthood by virtue of the spirituality they revealed, primarily through fasting and other food-centered behaviors such as multiplying food in miracles, exuding holy oils or milk from their own bodies, and giving food to the poor (Bynum 1987). Contemporary anorexics attempt to achieve perfection through self-control and thinness. They receive only pitying recognition from family, friends and medical professionals, and may die unless they find a path to the self-esteem, sense of control, and autonomy they so desperately seek through fasting (Bruch 1973, 1978; Lawrence 1984; Brumberg 1988).

Counihan explores how and why they do this and contrasts their behaviors with the fasting of women in other cultures and times. Clearly, were women to have other less destructive paths to power and autonomy, they would not need to undermine their very life force.

FOOD, MEANING AND GENDER

Maleness and femaleness in all cultures are associated with specific foods and rules controlling their consumption. For example, the Hua of New Guinea have elaborate conceptions about *koroko* and *hakeri'a* foods. The former are cold, wet, soft, fertile, fast-growing foods associated with females; the latter are hot dry, hard, infertile, and slow-growing foods associated with males. Women can become more like men by consuming *hakeri'a* foods; in particular these help minimize their menstrual flow. Men, on the other hand, proclaim publicly that female foods and substances are "not only disgusting but also dangerous to the development and maintenance of masculinity" but secretly eat foods associated with females to gain their vitality and power (Meigs 1984: xv and passim).

Between men and women, food is a means of differentiation as well as a channel of connection. By claiming different roles in regard to food and distinct attributes through identification with specific foods, men and women define their masculinity and femininity, their similarity and difference (see Pollock, this volume). In this volume, Kahn notes that men claim taro as their children and through nurturing and bearing taro-children, men emulate and counter-balance women's awesome reproductive power. Men and women use food and food metaphors to achieve the most intimate union as witnessed through language that equates eating with having sexual relations and through practices that equate the exchange of food with sexual intimacy, as do the Culina Indians (Pollock, this volume). Men can exert power over women by refusing to provide food or by refusing to eat or disparaging the food they have cooked. Women can also exert power over men by refusing to cook, controlling their food, or manipulating the status and meaning systems embodied in foods. As several of the essays here show, the exchange of food can be a way to mediate contested meanings and power relations between the sexes.

Class, ethnic and gender distinctions are also manifest through rules about eating and the ability to impose rules on others (Counihan 1992). For example, in United States culture thinness is valued. The dominant culture—manifest in advertising, fashion, and the media—projects a belief that thinness connotes control, power, wealth, competence, and success (Dyrenforth, Wooley and Wooley 1980). Research has revealed that obesity for women varies directly with class status and ethnicity. Greater wealth and whiteness go along with thinness; poor Puerto Rican, Black, and Native American women have lower status and greater obesity rates than well-off Euro-American women (Garb, Garb and Stunkard 1975; Stunkard 1977; Beller 1977; Massara and Stunkard 1979; Massara 1989; Sobal and Stunkard 1989). The standard of thinness upholds a class structure where men, whites, and the rich are superior to women, people of color, and the poor.

In more gender egalitarian cultures, we find either no information about body standards, or we find the same standards for both men and women. Young (1986: 117), for example, writes that for Melanesian peoples in Kalauna, "Corpulence is virtually unknown, and a small tight stomach is much admired; it is evidence of 'good' food and a restrained appetite." Whereas the Kalauna admire thinness, Polynesian peoples admire corpulence. Pollock (1992: 197) writes that "Large stature and a well-covered frame were also integral to the local view of a healthy individual. In Polynesian societies particularly, a well-covered individual was a good representative of his/her society." Neither group holds different standards for men and women as do many western societies, where observers have noted more stringent standards of thinness for women than for men even though women have greater biological propensity to be fat (Beller 1977). For Western women, dissatisfaction with their body size and shape is yet another expression of and contributor to their subordination, whereas in more gender equal cultures, women as well as men can find self-satisfaction through the body.

Attitudes towards food and body vary across cultures and provide a window into understanding gender identity and power, as do all foodways. The essays here address how men and women establish their relationships and social roles through food production, consumption and distribution. They explore how meanings and values surrounding food and eating define maleness and femaleness. They explore cultural variability in expressions of gender identity and power through foodways and open up discussions about the ramifications of that variability.

REFERENCES

Adams, Carol (1990). *The Sexual Politics of Meat: A Feminist-Vegetarian Critical Theory.* New York: Continuum.
Arnold, David (1988). *Famine: Social Crisis and Historical Change.* New York: Basil Blackwell.

Behar, Ruth (1989). Sexual Witchcraft, Colonialism, and Women's Powers: Views from the Mexican Inquisition. In *Sexuality and Marriage in Colonial Latin America*. Ed. Asunción Lavrin. Lincoln: University of Nebraska Press, pp. 178–206.

Bell, Rudolph M. (1985). *Holy Anorexia*. Chicago: University of Chicago.

Beller, Anne Scott (1977). *Fat and Thin: A Natural History of Obesity*. New York: Farrar, Straus, Giroux.

Bennett, John. (1943). Food and Social Status in a Rural Society. *American Sociological Review* 8, 5: 561–69.

Bruch, Hilde (1973). *Eating Disorders: Obesity, Anorexia Nervosa, and the Person Within*. New York: Basic Books.

Bruch, Hilde (1978). *The Golden Cage: The Enigma of Anorexia Nervosa*. New York: Vintage.

Brumberg, Joan Jacobs (1988). *Fasting Girls: the Emergence of Anorexia Nervosa as a Modern Disease*. Cambridge: Harvard University Press.

Bynum, Caroline Walker (1987). *Holy Feast and Holy Fast: The Religious Significance of Food to Medieval Women*. Berkeley: University of California Press.

Charles, Nickie and Marion Kerr (1988). *Women, Food and Families*. Manchester: Manchester University Press.

Chernin, Kim (1981). *The Obsession: Reflections on the Tyranny of Slenderness*. New York: Harper and Row.

Counihan, Carole M. (1988). Female Idenity, Food and Power in Contemporary Florence. *Anthropological Quarterly* 61, 2: 51–62.

Counihan, Carole M. (1992). Food Rules in the United States: Individualism, Control, and Hierarchy. *Anthropoloaical Quarterly* 65, 2: 55–66.

Détienne, Marcel and Jean-Pierre Vernant. (1989). *The Cuisine of Sacrifice among the Greeks*. Trans. Paula Wissing. Chicago: University of Chicago Press.

DeVault, Marjorie L. (1991). *Feeding the Family: The Social Organization of Caring as Gendered Work*. Chicago: University of Chicago Press.

Fitchen, Janet M. (1988). Hunger, Malnutrition and Poverty in the Contemporary United States: Some Observations on Their Social and Cultural Context. *Food and Foodways* 2, 3: 309–33.

Friedlander, Judith (1978). Aesthetics of Oppression: Traditional Arts of Women in Mexico. *Heresies* 1, 4: 3–9.

Garb, Jane L., J. R. Garb and A. J. Stunkard (1975). "Social Factors and Obesity in Navajo Children." *Proceedings of the First International Congress on Obesity*. London: Newman, pp. 37–39.

Goody, Jack (1982). *Cooking, Cuisine and Class: A Study in Comparative Sociology*. New York: Cambridge.

Kahn, Miriam (1986). *Always Hungry, Never Greedy: Food and the Expression of Gender in a Melanesian Society*. New York: Cambridge University Press.

Lappé, Frances Moore and Joseph Collins (1986). *World Hunger: Twelve Myths*. New York: Grove Press.

Lawrence, Marilyn (1984). *The Anorexic Experience*. London: Women's Press.

Leghorn, Lisa and Mary Roodkowsky (1977). *Who Really Starves? Women and World Hunger*. New York: Friendship Press.

Lewin, Kurt (1943). Forces behind Food Habits and Methods of Change. In *The Problem of Changing Food Habits*, Bulletin no. 108. Washington, DC: National Academy of Sciences, pp. 35–65.

Massara, Emily Bradley (1989). *Que Gordita. A Study of Weight Among Women in a Puerto Rican Community*. New York: AMS Press.

Massara, Emily B. and Albert J. Stunkard (1979). "A Method of Quantifying Cultural Ideals of Beauty and the Obese." *International Journal of Obesity* 3:149–52.

Mauss, Marcel (1967, orig. 1925). *The Gift: Forms and Functions of Exchange in Archaic Societies*. New York: Norton.

Meigs, Anna S. (1984). *Food, Sex and Pollution: A New Guinea Religion*. New Brunswick, NJ: Rutgers University Press.

Millman, Marcia (1980). *Such a Pretty Face: Being Fat in America*. New York: Norton.

Mintz, Sidney W. (1985). *Sweetness and Power: The Place of Sugar in Modern History*. New York: Penguin.

Moore, Henrietta L. (1988). *Feminism and Anthropology*. Minneapolis: University of Minnesota Press.

Ortner, Sherry B. (1978). *Sherpas Through their Rituals*. New York: Cambridge University Press.

Pollock, Nancy J. (1992). *These Roots Remain: Food Habits in Islands of the Central and Eastern Pacific since Western Contact*. Honolulu: Institute for Polynesian Studies.

Richards, Audrey I. (1932). *Hunger and Work in a Savage Tribe*. London: Routledge.

Richards, Audrey I. (1939). *Land, Labour and Diet in Northern Rhodesia: An Economic Study of the Bemba Tribe*. Oxford: Oxford University Press.

Sahlins, Marshall (1972). *Stone Age Economics*. Hawthorne, NY.: Aldine.

Siskind, Janet (1973). *To Hunt in the Morning*. New York: Oxford.

Sobal, Jeffery and Albert J. Stunkard (1989). Socioeconomic Status and Obesity: A Review of the Literature. *Psychological Bulletin* 105, 2: 260–275.

Stunkard, Albert J. (1977). Obesity and the Social Environment: Current Status, Future Prospects. *Annals of the New York Academy of Sciences* 300: 298–320.

Styles, Marvalene H. (1980). Soul, Black Women and Food. In *A Woman's Conflict, the Special Relationship between Women and Food*, Jane Rachel Kaplan, ed. Englewood Cliffs, NJ: Prentice-Hall, pp. 161–176.

Vaughn, Megan (1987). *The Story of an African Famine: Gender and Famine in Twentieth Century Malawi*. New York: Cambridge University Press.

Weismantel M. J. (1988). *Food, Gender and Poverty in the Ecuadorian Andes*. Philadelphia: University of Pennsylvania Press.

Young, Michael W. (1986). "'The Worst Disease:' the Cultural Definition of Hunger in Kalauna." In *Shared Wealth and Symbol: Food, Culture and Society in Oceania and Southeast Asia*, ed. Lenore Manderson. New York: Cambridge University Press.

FOOD AND SEXUAL IDENTITY AMONG THE CULINA

Donald K. Pollock

It is an ethnographic commonplace that food and sexual identity each may comprise richly fertile sources of metaphor for the other, a tropic potential that achieves exquisite proportions in areas such as the New Guinea highlands (e.g., Meigs 1984) and is perceptible if sometimes less apparently exotic in most cultures. Throughout the ethnographic region of lowland South America food and sexual identity similarly serve as two potentially productive codes, each "good to think" the other (e.g., Arcand 1978; Hugh-Jones 1978; Siskind 1973a: 88–129; Viveiros de Castro 1978; cf. Lévi-Strauss 1966).

The Culina Indians of western Amazonia consider the division of labor in food production to be one particularly important and "natural" conse-quence of sexual identity. In this article I examine how the Culina ration-alize this division of labor and how, in turn, food-productive activities serve as metaphors for sexual identity. Culina argue that neither men nor women can survive independently of each other, referring to both sub-sistence and procreation as processes ordered by necessarily opposed but complementary roles deriving from the fundamental characteristics of sex-ual identities. The mutually metaphorizing potential of food production and sexual identity rests upon this structural differentiation, which creates parallel but opposed categories of consumable substances/sexual identities. But beyond the facile correlation of food and sexual identity, expressed through their metaphoric counterpoint, the opposition between the quali-ties that order each domain is mediated by an ideology of exchange in which foods take on an essentially semiotic property to express the com-plementarity of sexual identities. In such contexts the material of food exchanges, while not entirely contingent, becomes reversible; sexual identity ceases to order the *production* of food. Rather, the complementarity of sexual identities is stressed in the regular exchange of opposed categories of food, in a sense without regard to the sexual identity of the producer(s).

In short, Culina view the relationship between food and sexual identity in much the way Lévi-Strauss viewed the nature of "totemic" systems (1963). At one level it is evident that characteristics of any category of food may be considered equivalent or related to a category of sexual identity. At this level categories in each domain are most obviously in metaphoric relation to each other. But at another level it is the opposition and complementarity of categories of food—or more broadly of the "natural" world as a whole—that serve as a model of and for the opposition and complementarity of categories of sexual identity. At this level the relation between categories of food and categories of sexual identity becomes largely irrelevant. It is the exchange of opposed and complementary categories of food by opposed and complementary categories of sexual identity that must be preserved.

The Culina are an Arawak-language-speaking group of perhaps 3000 individuals living in villages scattered along the major rivers of the Purus-Jurua region of western Brazil, with several villages in eastern Peru. This article is based on research conducted in the village called Maronaua on the Brazilian upper Purus River near the Peruvian frontier. Maronaua is a relatively large and complex village of some 150 individuals, most of whom have lived in this village since the early 1970s; before then the several groups comprising the current village led a peripatetic existence, following the movements of rubber-tapping camps along the Purus and Envira rivers, performing odd jobs in return for Brazilian manufactured goods. My analysis is restricted to Maronaua, where I conducted 12 months research in 1981–82; information available from other Culina local groups is largely consistent with my data, but variations introduce cautions in generalizing conclusions to all Culina. (See Adams 1962; 1963; 1971; 1976; Townsend and Adams 1978; and Rüf 1972 for information on Peruvian Culina.)

Among the Culina food transactions and exchanges take place in a variety of informal and formal contexts, from daily domestic production and consumption to elaborate ritual. To understand the place of foods in these contexts I first examine briefly what foods are and how they are produced.

Culina subsistence replicates, with minor variations, the pattern familiar among Amazonian groups, a pattern based on slash and burn horticulture combined with hunting, fishing, and gathering (Meggers 1971). The consumable substances produced through these means comprise the broad class of *tapari*, "food." From a dietary point of view manioc (*Manihot esculenta*) and plantains are the staple foods, as much as 60 to 70 percent of the bulk of any meal and an even larger proportion of the total daily dietary intake; nearly 80 percent of cultivated garden land is given over to manioc, plantains, and bananas. Meat may represent from 10 to 30 percent of the bulk of normal meals, and from day to day the amount of meat in the diet varies considerably.

Cultivated plants form the class of *dzamatapa* and include, in addition to manioc and plantains, corn, beans, rice, peanuts, squash, watermelon, sugar cane, and papaya. Many of them are seasonal, grown particularly from about April to October when the falling river level of the dry season exposes beaches on which they are grown. By about November these beaches begin to disappear under the rising river as the rainy season begins.[1] Gardens cut from the jungle surrounding the village are used principally for manioc and plantains, some sugar cane, a small amount of corn, occasionally pineapples, and a few potatoes.

Despite the prominence of cultivated foods in their diet, Culina consider meat, *bani*, to be the food par excellence; without meat, they say, they go hungry. Fortunately for the residents of Maronaua the nearby jungle has abundant game, and meat is almost always available in or from some household. The most common game animal (currently) is the collared peccary (*Tayassu tajacu*). A single hunter can usually count on killing at least one, and groups of hunters have killed up to 20 of these gregarious animals in a day. Other game animals include deer, tapir, white-lipped peccary, armadillo, paca, capybara, several monkeys, and a wide variety of birds. There are chickens, ducks, and a few domestic pigs in the village, but these are eaten only on rare occasions and are normally exchanged for other goods with passing traders. Many Culina men now own shotguns but are proficient hunters with the traditional bow and arrow to which they regularly turn when shotgun ammunition is scarce. An individual man hunts about every third day; Saturdays are given over to communal hunting in the dry season, while rainy season hunting is regularly communal.

Fish, *aba*, make up the third most common category of food in the diet. The Purus, and a lake near the village, produce numerous types of fish; Culina favor the giant catfish for its large quantity of virtually boneless flesh and the piranha for its flavor. As a relatively productive and easy task, fishing frequently serves as a break from the rigors of hunting, and on any given day one man in a household may fish while another hunts, insuring some catch for the household. However, fish are not considered to be "real" meat, and a steady diet of fish soon provokes complaints from household members.

Gathered foods are the least common in the Culina diet, and gathering appears to play only a minor role in the cycle of subsistence activities at Maronaua. A significant characteristic of most gathered foods is that they do not require cooking; mangoes, avocados, and various other fruits are eaten casually by those who care to seek them or when they are encountered on the way to gardens or hunting sites. The major exception is the fruit of the assai palm, called *hawa*. The *hawa* seed covering is boiled and may be sweetened with sugar to form a beverage. At least once or twice during the rainy season a collective gathering of *hawa* takes place, and the prepared drink is consumed communally.

The two major categories of Culina food, cultivated garden products, *dzamatapa*, and hunted game, *bani*, represent the basic female/male contributions to subsistence, and their production is ordered through a sexual division of labor that is in turn rationalized by reference to the qualities ascribed to such products and the transformations they undergo through cooking. This set of qualities also provides metaphors for sexual identity, as well as relations between sexual identities. Such relations operate at several levels; I begin by examining them through the tasks of daily subsistence.

The initial process of clearing forest for gardens and planting is a male activity. Clearing begins as the communal effort of all adult men of the village, who make a largely token show of collective force on the initial day of clearing, leaving the individual garden owner to complete the bulk of the work alone or with the assistance of a brother or son-in-law. The newly "slashed" garden is allowed to dry for about a month, at which time the owner burns off the dead and fallen undergrowth and small trees. After a few days the garden is planted. It is now a *widzaha*, a garden.

Husbands and wives own gardens jointly, but once a garden has been planted it becomes predominantly a domain of women. Women bear the responsibility for maintaining the gardens cleared and planted by their husbands, for weeding the undergrowth that continually springs up around plantings, and for collecting garden products. Men occasionally undertake to collect garden products, particularly manioc, but only in special ritual contexts. On a day-to-day basis it is common to see a couple returning from a garden, the wife laden down with a large basket of manioc or bananas, a machette in one hand, a child in the other, while her husband follows several yards behind burdened only by a single ripe banana he eats. The major exception to this rule finds men and women jointly collecting on cultivated beaches distant from the village, where the labor of men is felt to be necessary to speed the gathering, which can occupy a week or more of canoe paddling, of dozens of watermelons or large quantities of beans.

Hunting, by contrast, is the quintessential male activity, and meat is viewed as the primary male contribution to household subsistence. Men begin their hunting careers as small boys playing with miniature bows and arrows, shooting lizards and mice in the village to the warm approval of adults. Although men do not begin hunting regularly until marriage, an adolescent is judged as a prospective husband largely on his hunting skill, and any married man who fails to hunt regularly or successfully may be labeled "worthless," *tabakorata'i*, and may be compared to the vulture, who eats the meat others have killed. Hunting is the major preoccupation of adult men; gathering informally at least twice a day, their conversation invariably begins with or turns to hunting—a recent successful hunt is described in animated detail, or a future hunt is considered through speculation on the location of game.

Both men and women gather wild forest products, normally on a casual, individual basis. Women find various fruits or other plants on the way to gardens but rarely search beyond these well-worn paths. Men collect such plants while hunting, normally beyond the rough perimeter of gardens, and may make special trips to distant perennial sources of fruits or nuts. Most of these gathered products require no cooking and are eaten raw, and in general either men or women may collect any that is eaten raw, including cultivated sugar cane and papaya.

Both men and women fish, though women's fishing is normally restricted to the larger streams in the jungle near the village. These streams, and the river itself, are comparable to cultivated gardens. They are transitional zones between the social village and the unsocial jungle; fish are "mild" creatures appropriate for either sex to catch.

The initial domestic stage of these food-productive processes is cooking, normally an exclusively female task. Cooking as a skill and productive activity is valued in women as much as hunting skill is valued in men. Just as a poor hunter is considered "worthless," so too a woman who cooks poorly or infrequently is "worthless." The charge is rarely leveled against women, however, perhaps because cooking is a more or less daily activity that they cannot escape as easily as men can avoid or postpone hunting. Nonetheless, new wives are occasionally criticized for their neglect of this role; couples begin marriage living uxorilocally, and a new wife may be tempted to leave cooking duties to her mother.

From the Culina point of view this division of labor is rationalized in terms of qualities attributed to foods, qualities that make them appropriate for one sex or the other to collect or process. These qualities serve as general organizing principles of the world as a whole; those most relevant here are the relative "wildness" of foods, and their "smell."

In general the animals inhabiting the forest are considered wild, *wadita'i*, provoking fear, *nopine*, even in the men who hunt them regularly. As the domain of such animals, the forest itself becomes a fear-provoking place, particularly through its associations with the class of spirits called *tokorime*. The *tokorime* are, among other things, the spirits of animals; men may interact with such spirits in various contexts and indeed are transformed into *tokorime* as shamans. Women, on the other hand, interact with *tokorime* only in collective ritual settings in the secure social space of the village, and they risk unpleasant fates, including deformed babies and illness, if they encounter *tokorime* in the forest.

Animals, both forest and domestic (*odza bani*), are said to have strong, unpleasant smells, *maho badata'i*.[2] Cooking transforms unpleasant-smelling meat into good-smelling meat, that is, into edible food. Those animals which are not eaten, in general animals that are themselves meat-eating, "prohibited," *powadzama*, are considered to have the strongest and most unpleasant odor, impossible to mitigate through cooking.

Garden products, *dzamatapa*, are by contrast "mild," domesticated foods, just as gardens as social spaces are domesticated. Gardens begin as forest, and thus their creation is a task allocated to men, but once a garden has been planted its metaphorical and actual domestication makes it an area appropriate for women. Cultivated foods in general are "good-smelling," *maho bikata'i*, and the best of all are those sweet foods such as papaya and sugar cane which require no cooking. As a means of conceptually organizing subsistence labor, this system specifies that wild and strong-smelling substances, primarily game animals, are the domain of men, while "tame," mild- or good-smelling substances, primarily cultivated plants, are the domain of women. This principle operates consistently for substances that merge "wildness" and smell along the opposite axis as well. Tobacco, for example, is grown in gardens or occasionally within the village itself. Tobacco is domesticated and tame but is strong-smelling, unlike the other plants of cultivated gardens. As such, tobacco is grown and processed by men. Similarly, curative plants grow in the forest; they are wild but are good-smelling. As good-smelling substances they may be collected and "processed" by women, though men have more opportunities to locate curative plants on their hunts. By contrast, the jaboti tortoise (*Testudo tabulata*, in Culina *dzanikwa*), though a forest creature, is considered "tame"; indeed, it is caught alive and may be kept in the village where it eats "human" food, itself to be killed and eaten when other meat is not available. Because the jaboti is often found in or on the way to gardens and may live in the village, it is, one might say, metonymously social. As such, it is appropriate for women to "hunt" jaboti.

This system of qualitative attributes and the natural species it orders may be diagrammed as in Figure 1.[3]

The qualitative dimensions contrasting on the one hand "wild" and "tame" or domesticated plants and animals, and on the other "good" and "strong" or bad-smelling plants and animals, do not discriminate two pairs of neatly opposed categories of natural species. Rather, various species are ordered along the continua bounded by the contrastive qualities. At one set of extremes are found the most edible foods, sweet fruits and sugar cane for example, which require no cooking to be edible. At the opposite pole are wild, bad-smelling creatures such as the jaguar and vulture, which no amount of cooking will render edible. At the other set of extremes is found tobacco, a strong-smelling but domesticated plant that is "overcooked," burned to an ash to be consumed as snuff, which contrasts with the opposite pole where wild, good-smelling plants are found, plants that have curative properties and are masticated without cooking for use in illness treatment.[4]

Between these extremes lies the broad range of normal foods, including meat and most cultivated and gathered plants. Among these are two foods in particular that not only exemplify their consumable categories but also symbolize the subsistence productive contributions of men and women. The first is the white-lipped peccary, the *hidzama*. The *hidzama* occupies a special position as a wild, dangerous animal, yet one that is social and gregarious; it is both the most highly valued game animal and a symbol for

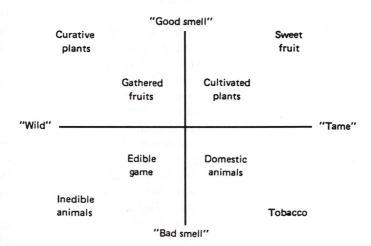

Figure 1   Classification of consumable substances.

Culina themselves. The second is the mildly fermented manioc beverage called *koidza*, prepared by boiling a mixture of premasticated cooked manioc and water. *Koidza* is doubly cooked and eaten; it is the metaphorical food of the *hidzama* in various ritual contexts. As exemplars of their food categories, *bani* and *dzamatapa* respectively, the *hidzama* and *koidza* serve as symbols of the male and female subsistence productive contributions, just as their contrastive qualities rationalize this division of subsistence labor.

This rationalization assigns to men and women the qualities attributed to the foods they produce. Men are wild like the animals they hunt and are associated with the jungle where such creatures live. Women are tame or social like the cultivated garden products they tend and collect. Humans all have a strong smell—which is why humans are *powadzama*, "prohibited" and inedible—but men in general are stronger-smelling than women. Adolescent boys are especially wild and strong-smelling, the metaphors here linking notions of unruly behavior and unrestrained sexuality in the liminality of the status; when an adolescent boy wishes to make himself attractive to a girl, he wears good-smelling leaves. Women may also become strong-smelling, particularly during menstruation and at childbirth; at such times they neither prepare food for their households nor eat with family members. Similarly, adolescent boys do not eat with their families but roam in small groups from household to household, eating freely and casually in each. Marriage has the effect of moderating these qualities for both men and women. Married men in particular lose the license for wild behavior they enjoyed as adolescents, and as the sexuality of both spouses becomes controlled at marriage they become tamer and milder-smelling. This effect is also produced through entering into the subsistence labor system of the household; marriage requires, but also is signaled by, the conceptual exchange of meat for garden products and of raw foods for cooked.[5]

This metaphorizing of marriage emerges clearly in the Culina myth of the origin of cultivated gardens. In this myth a husband and wife are hunting. She orders him to shoot her with an arrow, saying that she will become a garden. He kills her but is distraught and returns to his village. The next day he finds a garden where he had shot his wife. After several days the dead wife returns and is angered to discover that her husband has married her younger sister. She leaves, and the garden disappears. By the end of the myth the younger sister remarries, and the gardens reappear.[6]

The myth opens with both husband and wife hunting, perhaps less an improper redundancy or confusion of roles than an absence of properly differentiated roles. Two productive tasks are established: the husband hunts while his wife creates gardens. The killing of the wife to create a garden is, I believe, linked to the parallel process through which the *hidzama* peccary is created (discussed below) and draws upon the symbolism of sexual intercourse. The significance of marriage as the proper context for the linking of these dual roles is indicated both by the husband's need to find a new wife to tend the newly created garden when his first wife appears to die and by the dead wife's anger over her husband's marriage to her younger sister; he upsets the exchange by accepting his first wife's garden products but rejecting marriage with her. Being rejected as a wife in favor of her younger sister, she terminates the exchange by causing the gardens to disappear. Finally, the remarriage of the younger sister reestablishes the proper context for the subsistence exchange, and the gardens reappear.

Siskind has suggested that among the Sharanaua the predominant symbolic exchange between men and women is one of meat for sex (1973a: 88–109), a pattern she believes to be common in lowland South America as a whole (1973b). Although this meat-for-sex exchange may be at least potential in Culina metaphors of food and sex, in this group the exchanges between men and women are explicitly conceptualized as food for food: meat for cultivated garden products, *bani* for *dzamatapa*, *hidzama* for *koidza*.

The exchange character of these male/female relations provides one foundation for marriage and is a common principle on which households are defined as domestic groups through subsistence metaphors. This exchange character becomes even more overt in rituals, two of which may be described briefly.

The *dutse'e towi* or "order to get [something]" is a common ritualized demand made by women, "ordering" men to hunt, fish, or procure some other food. The most common form is the *dutse'e bani towi*, an "order to get meat." This process begins as village women go from household to household in the early morning, singing to the men in each that they are hungry, ordering them to hunt. Soon after the men leave on a collective hunting trip. During their absence each woman collects manioc from her gardens, from which she prepares the *koidza* beverage. The men return later in the afternoon, each man carrying a portion of the total catch. They are met by the women who form a rough line, singing to the men that they are hungry. The men drop their portions in front of the line, and the women scramble to grab a share, dividing the total roughly equitably so that those with large families get more. The men retire to their hammocks or go to bathe while the women prepare and cook the meat. Households cook individually, but when all is ready each woman brings her food to the headman's house, where the men gather to eat collectively. The meal is composed of two essential components: the meat brought by the men and the *koidza* prepared by the women.

The exchange character of this process is further marked on those occasions when the men of the village "order" the women to procure some food.[7] On one occasion a young man had killed two tapir at a distant hunting site but was unable to carry the heavy load of meat back to the village. The next day the men collectively sang from house to house, ordering the women to retrieve the meat. While the women were gone, each man collected manioc from his garden. The return of the women later in the day paralleled the normal process. The men formed a line and sang to the women as they arrived. The women dropped their portions in a pile before the men, who jumped to grab a share. While the women bathed, each man prepared a meal of the tapir meat and manioc, which was eaten communally by the women.

This reversal[8] of the normal *dutse'e towi* highlights critical aspects of the exchange. The role reversal was a source of amusement to everyone, but was justified on the grounds that when the women undertake to procure meat, it is their husbands' obligation to provide manioc and cook the meal. In this sense the reversal preserves the terms of the normal exchange: meat for garden products, raw foods for cooked. But the reversal was not complete: a man had killed the tapir, and though men collected the manioc they did not prepare *koidza* from it but served simply the boiled tubers. The differentially valued qualities that make women incapable of killing game animals also make men incapable of preparing proper *koidza*. *Bani* and *dzamatapa* may serve as symbols to be exchanged in either direction between men and women, but the production of material used in this symbolic mode remains anchored in the different qualities attributed to men and women.

During the dry season Culina occasionally perform a major ritual of the general variety known as *ehete*. Simplified versions of the *ehete*, consisting of singing and dancing, are performed often, but the more elaborate version of interest here occurs only two or three times in a season. The major feature of this ritual is the consumption of immense quantities of *koidza*, prepared several days in advance.[9] In the ritual the men retire to the jungle where they decorate themselves, while the women form a long line in the central ritual area of the village, each woman holding a pot of *koidza*. The men race into the village; they are said to represent the *hidzama* peccaries. The women "hunt" them by grabbing men and feeding them the *koidza*. Each man drinks a large quantity, leans on a wooden staff, and vomits up the drink. When the men have all been hunted, the women retreat to the jungle, and the men form a long line with the pots of *koidza*. The women charge into the village, again representing the *hidzama*, and are hunted by the men and fed the *koidza*. The women also vomit up the large quantity they consume.

The ritual and its symbolism are complex beyond this simplified summary and the scope of this analysis. But the ritual highlights the terms through which men and women interact, exemplified in this case as the *hidzama*, the most highly valued game animal, and the *koidza*, the quintessential garden product. As in the *dutse'e towi* the direction of the exchange may be reversed: women feed *koidza* to male peccaries, and vice versa. What is essential in these ritual contexts is not the production of materials that take on symbolic values, but the use of these symbols in exchange. That is, the link between sexual identities and specific categories of food becomes less important than the use of opposed but complementary categories of food in stressing the opposed but complementary nature of relations between sexual identities.

The Sharanaua studied by Siskind, neighbors of the Culina in Peru, have adopted a version of the *dutse'e towi* to which she refers as the "special hunt" (1973a: 96–104). The similarity to the Culina practice is evident; Sharanaua women even sing the appropriate songs in the Culina language. But the terms of the Sharanaua exchange differ. First, the exchange is individual rather than collective; an individual man hunts for an individual woman "partner," and she prepares and he eats the subsequent meal individually. Second, the exchange is overtly one of meat for sex; the successful hunter is granted sexual access to his woman partner, who may deny him sex if he fails to procure meat.

Rüf has reported a similar practice among the Culina at Zapote, a Peruvian village located near Siskind's Sharanaua (1972). These Culina arrange extramarital sexual liaisons between individual men and women during the collective singing that initiates the *dutse'e towi*. The Zapote Culina preserve the collective character of the process, however; men procure meat collectively, exchange it directly for cultivated and cooked foods, and eat collectively following the hunt. Sexual liaisons between arranged partners take place only later, after a second ritual that follows the *dutse'e towi* in a day or two.

Although the Culina at Maronaua do not incorporate this explicit sexual dimension in their *dutse'e towi,* the exchange of meat for garden products can become a metaphor for sexual relations. The myth of the origin of the *hidzama* peccary illustrates this potential.

According to this myth, otters proposed having sex with women in exchange for fish, an offer the women accepted. The men discovered their wives' infidelity and went to the stream posing as the women. The otters were fooled by the masquerade and brought the fish but were caught by the men hiding under the water. Later that day the women returned from their gardens with manioc to prepare *koidza*. One man demanded sex of his wife, but as she lay on her back in the house she saw the otter meat hanging from a rafter overhead. She jumped up, but before she could warn the other women the men grabbed them and killed them by blowing tobacco snuff into their nostrils. The women rose up, transformed into *hidzama* peccaries. The men poured out the *koidza* the women had prepared and chased away the peccaries, which fled into the jungle (cf. Adams 1962: 125–31).

The myth contains significant symbolic allusions, the most relevant here being those which refer to various exchanges. These are notably improper. Women offer sex for meat but to improper partners. Men offer meat for sex but with improper meat: Culina do not eat otter. The women offer *koidza*, but it is rejected by the men. The men offer sex, but it is rejected by the women. And so on.

In both this myth and that of the origin of gardens wives are transformed, in the one case into the *hidzama* and in the other into gardens. The myths reference a contrast between two types of transformations, those in which men create *hidzama* from the souls of the dead (in this case the women killed symbolically by tobacco) and gardens from jungle and those in which women create *dzamatapa* from gardens and consumable foods from raw substances. Moreover, the myths posit that relations between men and women in the context of marriage are metaphorically proper relations of subsistence production, and vice versa. And in both myths the proper terms of both subsistence and sexual relations are established through the rejection of various improper alternatives. The *hidzama* peccaries emerge to serve as the proper exchange for *koidza*, and this exchange in turn serves as the appropriate context for marriage and controlled sexual relations. In the previous myth, likewise and in more general terms, gardens emerge to serve as the proper exchange for hunted meat, a relation that is appropriate only in the context of marriage between the exchangers. The exchange is not directly one of meat for sex, as it appears to be among the Sharanaua. Rather, in life as in myth and ritual, the exchange of meat for garden products and marriage/sexual relations serve as metaphors for each other.[10]

The Culina division of food-productive labor might be considered to operate through a simple semiotic system in which consumable substances serve as icons of the contrasting sexual identities that produce them, just as a set of differences among consumable substances serves as a model of (and for?) a set of differences between sexual identities. Such a semiotic property entails several consequences. Sets of differences are not incommensurable; on the contrary, each is defined in terms of the other, and the limits of contrast are fixed by the opposed values of single predicates, "smell" and "wildness" being particularly relevant in this context. In this sense, sexual identities may be seen to differ because food-productive tasks differ, and vice versa. To perform such semiotic functions, symbols must exhibit an appropriate discreteness. Men may collect and cook manioc, but theoretically they cannot prepare it in its most consumable form as *koidza*. Similarly, women may hunt jaboti tortoises or fish, but theoretically they cannot hunt and kill the *hidzama* and other wild, strong-smelling game.[11] At the same time an interaction of symbols is implied by the interaction of sexual identities, which takes the form of an exchange or obligatory conjunction of different categories of consumable substances. Men and women are proper male and female persons not only because they produce the proper symbols but also because they exchange them properly; when women procure meat, men must preserve the symbolic exchange by procuring garden products.

Posing the relationship between food and sexual identity in these (perhaps metaphorically) semiotic terms grants a certain primacy or privileged "reality" to sexual identity as what is symbolized. I believe this describes the Culina view also; however food and sexual identity may serve as metaphors for each other, Culina take as given a fixity or immutability to sexual identity that is not ascribed to food-productive roles. Women are recognized as perfectly capable of shooting game, and men know exactly how to make *koidza,* but neither men nor women would lose their sexual identity by doing so. On the other hand, the critical qualities of these substances would be compromised by such reversals. To mention two hypothetical examples that informants described, tobacco snuff prepared by a woman loses its potency, while *koidza* prepared by a man would be too strong.[12]

This immutability of sexual identity, and something of the nature of the interaction of sexual identities viewed through subsistence metaphors, is suggested by Culina notions of sexual reproduction.

Sexual identity implies, for Culina, reproductive capacity. Although gender is fixed even before birth, and newborn infants are unambiguously recognized as male or female, the full implications of sexual identity, as opposed to gender, emerge only at puberty, when children leave the sexually undifferentiated status *ehedeni,* "child," and become adolescents. Boys are said to become *dzabitso* when they develop semen, *idzowiri.* Girls become *dzuato* with their first menses, *amade.* The acquisition of these adolescent statuses is marked by a simple ritual following which each becomes known by the appropriate status term.

Although semen and menstrual blood serve as signs of reproductive capacity, the Culina view of conception and infant development places greater stress upon a mother's breast milk, *dzohò*, as the female contribution to the process. A fetus is formed entirely of male semen, which collects in the womb, and repeated acts of sexual intercourse are necessary to "grow" a fetus. The pregnant woman makes no such contribution to the intrauterine development of the fetus. Rather, the mother's substantial contribution to the child's development begins at birth, when she begins to nurse the baby. The exclusively male process of fetal formation is replicated by the exclusively female process of infant nursing. Semen and milk are thus closely linked in Culina thought as comparable substances; the terms *idzowiri* and *dzoho* derive from the same root, *dzo*, the root of numerous terms referring to gastrointestinal processes and products, and semen is sometimes referred to as *dzoho tsueni*, "black milk," in opposition to the "white milk" of women.

Culina draw an explicit parallel between sexual procreation and garden creation. A man begins the "work" in each case, planting his semen as he does his garden. At birth the task becomes a female one; "growing" the child becomes the work of women just as gardens become the work of women when plantings emerge.

A more subtle symbolic significance attaches to food in the context of procreation. New parents are prohibited from eating the meat of male animals and various cultivated foods. Individuals may differ on precisely which animals and vegetable foods are to be avoided, but in all cases it is the male of the animal species and the "best-smelling" cultivated plants that are prohibited. To eat them would produce a variety of problems in the child, notably the illness called *epetuka'i*, said to be "like having a dung beetle in the abdomen."

Such food prohibitions may be viewed as indexes of the social status they signal (Fortes 1967: 10; Urban 1981) and also as establishing the boundaries of the relationships they define (Kracke 1981: 94); ideally any man who has contributed to the formation of a child through sexual relations with the mother is subject to these prohibitions at the birth of the child. Prohibited species that serve these functions are specified by reference to those attributes assigned to both foods and their human consumers. In this sense the prohibitions on meat and cultivated plants are rationalized in the same terms, but for different reasons. Such foods are transformed into bodily substance. The meat of male animals becomes equivalent to semen, both male substances that create humans. Newborn infants have an excess, so to speak, of such substance, being formed entirely of semen. Breast milk likewise becomes equivalent to cultivated foods, particularly good-smelling fruits that require no cooking. The female milk consumed by the nursing infant "balances" the male semen of which it was formed; to eat the best-smelling cultivated fruits would create an excess of such substance in the child, endangering its health.[13]

Violation of these food prohibitions produces an effect like having a dung beetle in the abdomen. The simile is appropriate if not lucid; the consequences are placed in the digestive system. Just as the dung beetle uses animal feces to block its burrow, so too the child's feces will harden and block his or her intestines.

These postpartum food restrictions broaden the nexus of relations among the producers and consumers of foods to include the newborn infant, and in doing so they prescribe with the sanction of illness the axial terms of the symbolic exchange of consumable substances. To be proper exemplars of sexual identity entails both that a man and woman provide semen and milk in the form of a child and additionally that they provide one another proper foods that avoid the extremes of the categories of consumable species. Procreation is one particularly focal product of sexual identity; the food exchanges that symbolize the process take on a comparable focal character.

This analysis has examined some of the ways in which food and sexual identity provide metaphors for each other. The link established between these otherwise distinct domains of Culina culture comprise a complex set of qualities ascribed to both foods and sexual identities, of which I have focused on two especially notable ones. These qualities are themselves metaphors through which Culina understand the cultural and "natural" worlds in which they live. I have stressed that while men and women are symbolically associated with distinct categories of consumable substances, meat versus garden products, strong-smelling versus mild-smelling species, semen versus milk, and so on, it is in many ways the interaction of such substances that defines proper sexual identities (and perhaps food itself) rather than the simple production of these foods. When Culina assert that men and women cannot live without each other they are proposing precisely this: it is the constant exchange of the properties embodied in foods and sexual identities through which natural species, humans, and ultimately Culina culture itself emerge.

NOTES

An earlier version of this paper was read at the South American Indian Conference at Bennington College in August 1983. I am grateful to the participants of that conference for their comments and suggestions. Carole Counihan also provided numerous invaluable comments and suggestions for improving my initial rough efforts.

 1. Dried corn and beans may be found in the village for some months after the end of the dry season but are not favored as foods. Some dried corn is eaten but is most often fed to chickens, and the bulk of dried beans is sold to passing Brazilian and Peruvian traders.
 2. Culina have a generous vocabulary for smells, virtually a taxonomy, which I simplify here into a single dimension.
 3. This rendering should not be read as a complete analysis of Culina modes of classification; it is simplified and reflects only the two dimensions especially relevant in the present context.
 4. Lévi-Strauss's analysis of South American Indian myth (e.g., 1973) raises the question of the place of honey in this system. Honey falls, with curative plants, near the extremes of wildness (being produced by creatures that fall into the Culina category "poisonous things") and good smell. I have selected curative plants rather than honey to exemplify this category, however, as such plants are linked to tobacco, both substances used in illness treatment. Honey more properly contrasts with hot peppers.
 5. The metaphors through which Culina consider sexual identity have relevance for the current debate in which women are presumed to be universally considered "natural" beings while men are "cultural" (e.g., Ortner 1974; MacCormack and Strathern 1980). Although the issue is beyond the more limited scope of this article, it will be obvious that for Culina, men have distinct "natural" associations, while women are more "social." In any case, such labels do not precisely capture the Culina view of either sexual identity or personhood, nor are such associations used by Culina to justify male domination of women.
 6. Adams (1962: 140–50) presents fuller versions of this myth, which I summarize here.
 7. I consider the *dutse'e towi* in which women "order" men to be the normal one, as the reversal in which men "order" women is less common and irregularly performed in Maronaua. However, Adams suggests that in the village of San Bernardo the reversal regularly follows the normal *dutse'e towi* (Adams 1962: 95).
 8. This example is actually a double reversal; not only did the men order the women to procure food, the women procured meat. Normally the men would order the women to collect manioc, bananas, or some other appropriately female food item.
 9. Townsend and Adams refer to this special variety as *wabui porini* (1978). This term is not used in Maronaua, to my knowledge. *Wabui* is a type of log with a porous, soft wood; it is hollowed out to make a large vessel for the *koidza*. *Wabui porini* would mean, roughly, "*wabui* log laying down."
10. Lévi-Strauss (1969: 83–108) discusses a group of myths concerning the origin of "wild pigs," including a Bororo myth with close similarities to that of the Culina (p. 94). His suggestion that myths about the origin of cooking and the origin of pigs are structurally isomorphic (p. 97) seems consistent with the Culina use of both game animals and garden products to establish distinct but complementary productive roles.
11. At a further extreme, women risk harm even by seeing "prohibited" (*powadzama*) species in the jungle, while men may see and kill them. Of most of these species it is supposed that men can even eat them without harmful consequences, though none, of course, would want to.
12. I regret that my data do not include information on the actual or hypothetical killing of game by women.
13. The food preparation and eating restrictions placed on menstruating women operate in reverse, menstrual blood is an extremely "strong-smelling" substance, which would transform the smell of cooked food from mild to strong, rendering it inedible.

REFERENCES

Adams, P. (1962). "Textos Culina." *Folklore americano* 10: 93–222.
———. (1963). "Some Notes on the Material Culture of the Culina Indians." *Antropologica* 12: 27–44.
———. (1971). "La cultura del grupo idiomático Culina." Mimeo. Summer Institute of Linguistics, Lima, Peru.
———. (1976). "Cerámica Culina." *Peru indigena* 10 (24–25): 82–87.
Arcand, Bernard (1978). "Making Love is like Eating Honey or Sweet Fruit, It Causes Cavities: An Essay on Cuiva Symbolism" In Erik Schwimmer, ed. *The Yearbook of Symbolic Anthropology*, pp. 1–10. Montreal: McGill-Queen's University Press.
Fortes, Meyer (1967). "Totem and Taboo." *Proceedings of the Royal Anthropological Institute for 1966*, pp. 5–22.
Hugh-Jones, Christine (1978). "Food for Thought: Patterns of Production and Consumption in Pira-Parana Society." In J. S. La Fontaine, ed. *Sex and Age as Principles of Social Differentiation*, pp. 41–68. New York: Academic Press.
Kracke, Waud (1981). "Don't Let the Piranha Bite Your Liver: A Psychoanalytic Approach to Kagwahiv (Tupi) Food Taboos." In Kenneth Kensinger and Kracke, eds. *Food Taboos in Lowland South America*, pp. 91–142. Working Papers on South American Indians 3. Bennington College.
Lévi-Strauss, Claude (1963). *Totemism*. Boston: Beacon Press.
———. (1966). *The Savage Mind*. Chicago: University of Chicago Press.
———. (1969). *The Raw and the Cooked*. New York: Harper & Row.
———. (1973). *From Honey to Ashes*, New York: Harper & Row.
MacCormack, Carol, and Marilyn Strathern, eds. (1980). *Nature, Culture and Gender*. Cambridge: Cambridge University Press.
Meggers, Betty (1971). *Amazonia*. Chicago: Aldine.
Meigs, Anna S. (1984). *Food, Sex, and Pollution*. New Brunswick: Rutgers University Press.
Ortner, Sherry B. (1974). "Is Female to Male as Nature Is to Culture?" In M. Z. Rosaldo and L. Lamphere, eds. *Woman, Culture, and Society*, pp. 67–87. Stanford: Stanford University Press.
Rüf, Isabelle (1972). "Le 'dutsee tui' chez les Indiens Culina du Pérou." *Bulletin de la société suisse des américanistes* 36: 73–80.
Siskind, Janet (1973a). *To Hunt in the Morning*. New York: Oxford University Press.
———. (1973b). "Tropical Forest Hunters and the Economy of Sex." In D. Gross, ed. *Peoples and Cultures of Native South America*, pp. 226–40. New York: Doubleday.
Townsend, Patricia, and P. Adams (1978). "Estructura y conflicto en el matrimónio de los Indios Culina de la Amazonia peruana." *Communidades y culturas peruanas*, pp. 139–60.
Urban, Gregory (1981). "The Semiotics of Tabooed Food: Shokleng (Ge)." In Kenneth Kensinger and Waud Kracke, eds. *Food Taboos in Lowland South America*, pp. 76–80. Working Papers on South American Indians 3. Bennington College.
Viveiros de Castro, Eduardo (1978). "Alguns aspectos do pensamento Yawalapiti (Alto Xingu): Classificações e transformações." *Boletim do Museu Nacional*, Antropologia n.s. 26. Rio de Janeiro.

"MEN ARE TARO" (THEY CANNOT BE RICE): POLITICAL ASPECTS OF FOOD CHOICES IN WAMIRA, PAPUA NEW GUINEA

Miriam Kahn

Pacific Islanders have been increasingly exposed to such Western imports as rice, canned meat and fish, and sugar. With the arrival of each new food comes the need to make a choice between the old and the new. The Wamira people of Papua New Guinea, who have access to both traditional and imported foods, make definite cultural choices between the two. The decision not to replace taro or yams with a Western import may be as revealing as the decision to buy a package of rice. In this article I examine the contexts of and reasons for such choices among Wamirans.

Most studies of the use of imported foods in the Pacific sidestep the issue of choice and deal instead with its consequences, a topic in itself of great significance (e.g., Buchbinder 1977; Coyne 1981; Parkinson 1982; Thaman 1982; and Grant 1988). Thus analyses of dietary changes and their consequences (whether nutritional, ecological, or cultural) have generally neglected the aspect of choice—how and why decisions are made. Furthermore, though many authors have discussed the sociopolitical significance of traditional foods in Oceania, especially in Melanesia (among them Bell 1946; Hogbin 1970; Kahn 1986; Lea 1969; Meigs 1984; Powdermaker 1932; Spriggs 1980; Tuzin 1972; and Young 1971), few have studied the contemporary persistence of traditional foods. Only by examining the juxtaposition, supplementation, and replacement of traditional foods with imports, and by analyzing when and why each category is used, exchanged, and eaten, can one adequately address the question of choice.

I begin to rectify this imbalance by analyzing feasts in the village of Wamira, Papua New Guinea, examining the contexts and motives of these people for using traditional foods or replacing them with imports.[1] I focus specifically on feast behavior because feasts are ceremonial occasions when cultural themes and values come to the fore more vividly than in everyday eating behavior.

Feasts among the Wamira come in two analytical categories, "social" and "political." Social feasts celebrate occasions that are relatively free of political competition and tension. They emphasize relationships of solidarity and incorporation. At such times food is shared and eaten communally in a comparatively relaxed atmosphere. Political feasts, on the other hand, occur when rivalries and tensions among men are greatest, when fear of sorcery among competitors is rife, and when, as a result, the need for social control in the form of recognized leadership is most pronounced. Because political exchanges allow conflicts to be acted out—and indeed, may be generated by conflict—they emphasize differences between individuals and groups rather than solidarity among them. At political feasts, food is exchanged with elaborate and calculated ritual. It is not eaten communally; either it is consumed by separate groups of people, or it is carried away by them to be eaten in private.

In Wamira, social feasts do not require specific foods to communicate the message of solidarity. The sharing of food, whether rice, canned meat, or traditional fare, is symbolically sufficient to express the message of social cooperation. As a result, Western foods, which can be obtained with less labor, have become convenient substitutes and supplements for arduously produced traditional foods. Political feasts, on the other hand, require traditional foods, especially taro, in addition to whatever imported food is served. Wamiran men identify with their taro, which carries important symbolic messages about their status and is used to manipulate relationships between them. At those times when male rivalries must be resolved and leadership must be reinstated and communicated, taro, which of all foods is alone capable of symbolically communicating male status and virility, must be exchanged. Rice will not do.

TARO: THE POLITICAL SIGNIFICANCE
OF "REAL FOOD"

Wamira, a village of about four hundred Wedau-speaking people, is located on the northern coast of southeastern Papua New Guinea (see Figure 1). Its five hundred hectares are bounded on the north by Goodenough Bay,

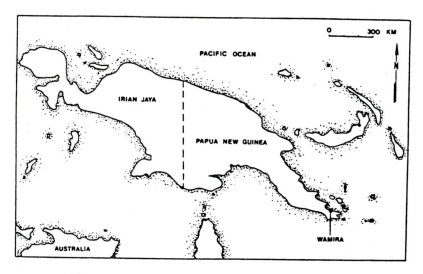

Figure 1   Location of Wamira within Papua New Guinea.

on the east and west by two rivers, and on the south by mountains that rise further inland to become the precipitous peaks of the Owen Stanley Range. The mountainous terrain behind the village forms a rain barrier that extends for some thirty kilometers along the coast. As a result, Wamira and several other coastal villages suffer from an unusually dry climate. Rainfall is approximately 1300 millimeters a year.[2] The dry season is particularly long, lasting for eight months from April through November. The limited rainfall, and the resultant grassy vegetation, make horticultural production (the main source of subsistence) in Wamira more laborious than in other, more tropical parts of the country. In contrast to their fellow Papua New Guineans, who cultivate plots by slash-and-burn techniques, Wamirans must cultivate gardens in the savanna, where the stoloniferous roots of the grass (*Imperata cylindrica*) render work extremely difficult. Moreover, Wamirans must irrigate their taro gardens, because rainfall is insufficient for the proper growth of the tubers.[3] Thus the cultivation of taro, their most prized traditional crop, is anything but easy.

Although taro (*Colocasia esculenta*) is only 20 percent of the diet, it is the main crop of political and ritual importance. Wamirans divide their food world into two categories: *lam* and *tia*. *Lam*, the general category of vegetable food, is also the word for the vegetable food par excellence, taro. *Tia* is the accompaniment for *lam*. *Lam* on its own may constitute a meal; *tia* on its own would not. According to Wamirans, only taro is "real food." In contrast to all other edibles, it fills them up and "sits in the stomach like stone." Wamirans say they can eat a lot of other foods, whether traditional or introduced, yet still remain hungry.

Preference and respect for taro go beyond any nutritional qualities the tubers possess. Taro stands apart from other foods because it alone carries symbolic meanings and messages about Wamiran men, and it is used to communicate the nuances of their relationships with one another. Because of their ability to produce children and to transfer matrilineal substance (*dam*), women are perceived as naturally creative and reproductive beings. Men, on the other hand, are respected as creators and producers in the horticultural realm. Through the use of personal magic, men channel their creative energy into the production of taro.

Taro is viewed by Wamirans as a human surrogate (Kahn 1986). Like human beings, the growing taro corms are believed to possess the ability to talk, hear, see, and smell. With their ears, for example, the taro hear the magic chanted to them during cultivation. With their noses, they sensitively smell out those substances such as grease, soap, oil, and traces of meat on a person's breath which are thought to be inimical to their growth. Taro are believed to exist in male and female forms; male taro regenerate only themselves, whereas female taro put out several offshoots called "children." Likewise, the regenerative stalks of taro are likened to umbilical cords (*vegavega*).

Human properties are believed to reside in the entire taro plant as long as the stalks are attached. As soon as taro corms are destalked, however, human properties are relocated in the stalks alone. Thus there is a significant symbolic difference between presenting bundled taro with the stalks attached and presenting taro in the form of severed corms. Bundles of taro with their stalks are called *diwara*. Only men may present and exchange them, and they do so at political feasts. Loose taro corms may be exchanged by women, who offer them at social feasts. One man explained the sexual association to me: "Men are bundled taro; women are only garden baskets" (which are used for carrying loose taro and other vegetable foods). In the final display of harvested taro at political feasts, men flaunt their virility, communicate their social standing and power, and settle conflicts and rivalries in their relationships with one another. After the harvest display, men retrieve the regenerative stalks (which they call their "seeds") from the taro they presented. A man's reproductive identity is linked to these seeds. As Lévi-Strauss has noted for Melanesia, men may "exchange women but refuse to exchange seeds" (1966: 110).

THE ARRIVAL OF RICE AND CANNED FISH

Contact between Wamira and the Western world started in 1891, when the first Anglican missionaries arrived at the shore near Wamira. Since then villagers' lives have been affected greatly, first by the mission, more recently by government employees. Indeed, Wamirans live less than an hour's walk (about three kilometers) from Dogura, a sizable and influential mission station that serves as headquarters of the Anglican mission in Papua New Guinea (Kahn 1983). Wamirans adapted easily to Christianity in several ways, and warfare and cannibalism ended soon after contact. Wamirans, who now are all baptized and take Christian names, celebrate religious holidays with exuberance. On Sundays they occasionally go to church. All but the most elderly women wear Western clothing.

World War II, and the national government since independence in 1975, have brought more material changes to Wamira. Corrugated iron roofs are rapidly replacing traditional grass thatch. Western items, such as radios, tape decks, and furniture, increasingly find their way into Wamiran homes. Even the Wamirans' irrigation aqueduct, originally constructed of hollowed logs, is now a government-financed metal pipe.

One result of contact and the subsequent exposure to Western goods is a perceived need for cash. Because the dry climate prohibits the ready development of cash crops, Wamirans have little means by which to earn money within the village. Copra, the only cash crop available, requires strenuous work for minimal economic return. Garden produce, which Wamirans sell at the local market in Dogura, brings in only a small amount of pocket money. The main way to acquire cash is to leave the village for work in towns. Their long contact with outsiders, their exposure to Western ways and education, has given many Wamirans a rudimentary knowledge of English, and villagers are able to secure decent jobs on wharfs or in stores, banks, hotels, hospitals, and schools. In fact, two-thirds of the total Wamiran population in Papua New Guinea resides in towns; only one-third lives in the village. Thus cash enters the village primarily in the form of remittances sent by relatives working in urban areas.

Cash is used to purchase trade store items such as kerosene, tobacco, and, of course, food. Dogura has a large, well-stocked trade store. Other, smaller stores spring up in the village (and occasionally collapse soon thereafter) whenever an enterprising family pools its resources and energy. Approximately 45 percent of the money spent in these stores is used to purchase food. Most of the rest goes on kerosene and tobacco. The foods Wamirans purchase most frequently are sugar, rice, canned fish, canned meat, tea, and hard biscuits (in that order). In 1977 a family of four spent an average of five kina (U.S. $4.30 at the time) a week on imported food. By 1982, when I last lived in Wamira, the amount was approximately twice as much.[4] Judging from reports I received in letters in 1987, the amount is almost four times what it was in 1977. The amount villagers spend on imported foods has quadrupled in the past ten years.

THE LANGUAGE OF FEASTS

This brief ethnographic background highlights the traditional importance of taro and the contemporary availability of cash and imported foods. What are the implications for feasts? I perceive Wamiran feasts, elaborate ceremonies during which food commemorates, celebrates, and communicates sociopolitical concerns, as falling into two categories that correspond to the two major modalities of exchange identified by Barth (1966) and discussed in detail by Paine (1976), namely incorporation and transaction. I refer to them as "social" and "political" respectively. A *social exchange* signifies a relationship of solidarity and incorporation for the group. In such an exchange, individual interests are identical. Free of the notion of competition, individuals strive for co-identity. Their strategies are directed toward maximizing the sum of the individuals' assets. A *political exchange*, on the other hand, presents an opportunity for acting out conflict and, in fact, is often generated by conflict. It emphasizes boundaries between groups and differences among group members. Social control is maintained by individuals. Whereas a social exchange accentuates loss of personal autonomy in return for a heightened sense of group identity, a political exchange negates a sense of group identity and allows for more personal autonomy. Both types of exchanges are equally necessary in Wamira, where there is an emphasis on balancing individual interests with those of the group (Kahn 1986).

From his work on Goodenough Island, Young also notes distinctions between various types of food exchanges (Young 1971). He proposes three, not two, categories, which correspond to dimensions of social proximity. Young's description sheds light on the emotional tone of different types of feasts. Barth's transaction mode, Young's third category of enemy, and my political category all correspond to one another.

> Stated crudely, there are distinctions to be made between food given and received in a kinship context, in an affinal context, and in a context external to these, which may be labeled "political." The last is the realm of "enemies." Food is welcomed as nurturing in the first context, accepted as satisfying in the second, and feared as shaming in the last. The first is given informally and received willingly, the second is given modestly

and received diffidently, and the last is given aggressively and received with reluctance which is dissimulated by a show of indifference (Young 1971: 195).

Each type of exchange, whether social or political, has its specific characteristics, particular meaning attributed to the accompanying behavior, and
contexts in which it is appropriate. As Paine states, "It may be expected
that [these] modes of exchange, as ideal propositions about relationships,
will each have its typical code, and this will be an instrument of the mode
of social control prevailing in the relationship" (Paine 1976: 73).

In Wamira, the characteristics of each type of feast are clearly stipu-
lated. Social feasts never include pork. Taro, if presented, is given only in
the form of loose corms. Any other food may be included; one's choice
may in part be determined by what food is in season at the time of the
feast. The manner of distributing and eating the food is also explicitly
defined. After the food is amassed, everyone unites to prepare and cook it.
The cooked food is then distributed according to age or gender groups—
but not along lines of patrifiliation—and is eaten in public.

Political feasts must include pork as well as *diwara*. Only after the food
has been ceremonially displayed is the pig killed and butchered and the
taro corms severed from their stalks. While still raw, the food is distributed to groups that are defined along lines of patrifiliation, that is, resi-
dence/garden groups. The recipients either carry their portions of raw food
home with them to cook and eat privately or else stay at the feast site but
remain in separate groups to cook and eat.

The different behaviors appropriate for each type of feast are highly
symbolic. As mentioned, food is distributed according to age or gender
groups at social feasts and according to patrifiliated groups at political
feasts. Patrifiliated groups of residence or gardening units harbor tension;
groups defined by age or gender are relatively tension-free. Whether food
is cooked communally, as at social feasts, or carried away while still raw,
as at political feasts, also is significant. The act of cooking with others
indicates an absence of fear of sorcery. To carry food away, however, is to
indicate fear of sorcery and/or poison.

Likewise, the choice between "eating together" and "eating separately"
has symbolic import. To eat together is to indicate openness and trust.
Analyzed linguistically, it suggests a sense of production and accom-
plishment. "To eat together" is called *am gogona*. The term is derived
from the word *am* "to eat," and *gogona*, the adverbial form of the verb
gogo "to sprout," "to grow," or "to rise." Conversely, "to eat separately"
indicates distrust and antagonism. Its etymology implies a sense of poverty.
"To separate" is *vilamonei*, the verb formed from the noun *lamolamona*,

a poverty-stricken beggar, usually with neither possessions nor kin. Thus eating together, as in social feasts, implies trust, cooperation, and production. Eating separately, behavior appropriate for political feasts, implies suspicion, enmity, and poverty.

The contexts in which Wamirans decide to hold one or the other type of feast are likewise distinct. Social feasts are held to "restore strength" following communal labor (such as on irrigation canals, on a house, or on the village school), to welcome an individual returning to the village after a long sojourn in town, and to celebrate events observed by Westerners (such as church activities, birthdays, and Christmas). Political feasts celebrate stages in the life cycle, such as marriages and deaths (when women's roles in the maintenance and manipulation of matrilineal substance come to the fore), and mark major stages in the cultivation of taro, such as turning the sod for a new garden, planting, and harvesting tubers (accomplishments in the creative and productive activities of men). To a Wamiran, the male horticultural activities of preparing the sod, planting, and harvesting correspond most directly to the female role in reproducing society. Therefore, they are also the stages in the horticultural cycle when male competition and suspicion mount, and when it is of utmost importance to define and control the social order. At these times leadership, as an acknowledged form of social control, is easily threatened and must be commandingly reinstated. Leadership is reaffirmed symbolically through the display and exchange of *diwara* among men.

SOCIAL FEASTS: OF FRIED CHICKEN AND BIRTHDAY PARTIES

The following two social feasts occurred in 1977. They serve to illustrate the general characteristics, meanings, and contexts of an incorporation type of feast.

One feast was held to "restore the strength" of workers after they had cleaned out an irrigation canal (which, unlike turning the sod, planting, or harvesting, is considered only a minor horticultural stage). In Wamira all men using a common canal must cooperate in its construction and maintenance. Maintenance involves cleaning out the grass that has sprouted since the canal was last in use and deepening the eroded channel. In this particular case, about thirty men united to do the work. While they cleared and restored the long canal, the women of their households energetically prepared food that had been contributed earlier in the day by all the families engaged in the communal task. Each family contributed a garden basket of vegetable food, consisting primarily of loose taro corms, plantains, bread-fruit, and sweet potatoes. In addition, three bags of rice (5 kg each), two cans of fish, two bags of sugar (1 kg each), and three boxes of tea were supplied by families able to afford the contribution of purchased food.

While men were busy working, women carried the food, cooking pots, and plates to the river. There they washed the pots and prepared the food amid boisterous joking and laughter. At such times of communal labor and social feasting, jovial banter fills the air. A typical joke revolves around what Wamirans perceive as their natural and uncontrollable state of greed. For example, while several of the women were gone collecting firewood, one young woman who remained behind joked to her three friends about how they should abscond with the bags of rice, cans of fish, tea, and sugar, and enjoy a private picnic.

By the time the men were finished with their work and had arrived at the scene of the feast, the women had prepared four pots of rice and eight pots of traditional foods. The food was divided into two equal groups, one of which was given to the men and the other to the women. It was further divided into equal portions, each portion going to an individual. Everyone sat down and ate together. When they were finished, one man rose and briefly addressed the crowd: "Today everyone came to help with the work. That is good. We worked together and we ate together." The feastly gathering confirmed their solidarity, friendship, and cooperative spirit. The atmosphere was relaxed and jovial. Everyone had pitched in to work, each individual received an equal share of food, and all ate together.

Another social feast occurred when a man gave a birthday party for his six-year-old daughter. On the day of the party, every household in the hamlet brought a contribution of food, almost exclusively breadfruit, which was in season at the time. Everyone in the hamlet sat down together and cooked the food. Twenty-four children were present, all dressed in their church-going best. Two young men wrapped colorful cotton "laplaps" around their waists, adorned their hair with flowers, and acted as waiters. The food contributed by the girl's father was set out in dishes on a table that had been decorated with a tablecloth and flowers. The display consisted of crackers with smoked oysters (from a can), rice, fried chicken, canned beef spiced with curry, bread, butter, and jam. There was also a birthday cake (baked by me) and a large dish of fresh pineapple with canned cream.

As the invited guests eagerly ate their helpings of both the breadfruit and the Western imports, a man of relatively high status stood up and educated them about the friendly nature of the gathering. "This party is called a 'birthday party,'" he said. "Unlike other feasts [i.e., of the political sort], you have to sit here and finish the food. You cannot take it home with you." Dutifully, they all sat and ate together.

This feast, like the one after the irrigation work, expressed commensality and communality. People ate together in a sociable and tension-free atmosphere. In both feasts the message of friendship and cooperation was communicated by the sharing of food, whether breadfruit, rice, taro corms, or smoked oysters on crackers.[5] The symbolic statement made at such social feasts is quite different from that made at political feasts.

POLITICAL FEASTS: OF TARO AND MEN

Before describing and analyzing political feasts, it is necessary to say a word about Wamiran leadership. Each of the eighteen patrilocal hamlets in the village has one acknowledged leader. Yet relationships among hamlet men are not immutable. The leader surpasses other men only slightly in terms of wealth (mainly pigs, taro, and taro magic). The leader's primary power, which rests in but is not guaranteed by his genealogical status of patrilineal primogeniture, must be continually reconfirmed.

A leader achieves respect through his ability to organize and unify his group and expresses his leadership through the manipulation of food at feasts. His group consists of smaller antagonistic hamlet divisions, each of which also has its own genealogically ascribed leader of slightly lesser status than the hamlet leader. The presence of these aspiring competitors challenges a leader's powers and makes his task of unifying the group difficult. Rivalries and conflicts among minor leaders usually threaten to erupt during the process of taro cultivation, an activity in which male powers are especially at stake. Male solidarity is necessary not only for technological reasons but also as a symbolic statement of hamlet amity and to dispel fears of sorcery. Group cooperation and harmony are seen as direct reflections of the leader's powers and of his ability to manipulate human relationships through the use of food. In Wamiran terminology, "If the leader is weak the group falls, if he is strong and is a real man the group unites and works."

The following two examples of political feasts took place in the hamlet of Inibuena. The acknowledged leader, Jeremiah, was the firstborn son in a line of firstborn sons for several generations. His rivals within the hamlet were Osborne, Malcolm, and, to a lesser degree, Simon.

In July 1977 the men of Inibuena began turning the sod to make new taro gardens, a stage of production that is riddled with competition, distrust, and sorcery. For several nights preceding their work they held séance-like hamlet meetings at which they tried to allay their anxieties about producing abundant, robust taro and about the jealousy and sorcery that prosperity elicits. Their discussion at one such meeting was as follows.

Jeremiah: Tomorrow, before we begin our work, we'll eat together. Bring your "sweet potatoes" [a euphemism for taro]. After we eat, we'll discuss the work.

Copland King (Jeremiah's younger brother): I was sleeping and I dreamed that everything will be "all right" [harmonious and sorcery-free] among us. Men will not "fall" [die from sorcery].

Jeremiah: I, too, dreamed everything will be all right. But to have three leaders [himself, Malcolm, and Osborne] is no good. One is good. If you get sick or "get the feeling" [that you have been attacked by sorcery], put your work aside. Magical substance is in our presence. Tomorrow we'll eat together and then we'll begin our work. We won't become prosperous [produce so much food that it will cause jealousy and sorcery]. Later we'll have a big feast [to indicate successful, trouble-free completion of the gardening process].

Before the men began to turn the sod, the hamlet members held the feast at which they distributed pork and *diwara*. People contributed food as separate households. Jeremiah brought the pig. Malcolm, Osborne, and Simon, those individuals most threatening to Jeremiah, and of whose support Jeremiah needed to be reassured, each proudly arrived with a *diwara*. Other households contributed stalks of plantains, a few yams, and sweet potatoes. Three of the households were headed by women (widows or women separated from their husbands) who brought their food, either loose taro corms or yams, in a garden basket.

Malcolm, Osborne, and Simon took charge of the food distribution. They first filled a garden basket with some of the raw vegetable food and carried it and a chicken (given by Malcolm) to Jeremiah. They did so because a leader is not allowed to handle food at a distribution. Abstemious behavior is said to indicate self-control and lack of greed and, thus, extraordinary powers.

The same three men then divided the rest of the raw food into equal portions that were presented to hamlet members according to patrilocal residential divisions. Within each residential group, the food was further divided into equal portions according to households. Everyone gathered in groups according to hamlet divisions, and within these divisions according to households. They prepared their vegetables and cooked them with their pork, remaining in separate groups to eat.

A more analytical review of the feast helps unravel the messages communicated about hamlet dynamics. The exchange encompassed two components, each of which confirmed a different aspect of the social order. First, there was an exchange between the leader and the hamlet members. Jeremiah gave the people a pig. In return, the people supplied him with vegetable foods, especially taro and plantains, plus a chicken because he could not eat his own pork. In short, he gave them meat, which they repaid with vegetable food. This exchange symbolically confirmed support of and obedience to one leader. Second, there was a unifying exchange among the households within the hamlet. Each household gave a contribution, several of which were unequal in quality and quantity. Yet in return, each household received an equal share. Thus, hamlet harmony and cohesion were also established. Within the hamlet, moreover, individual men had a chance to express status differences. For example, the three rival leaders presented *diwara*, whereas the others provided plantains. Gender distinctions were communicated as well. Men presented *diwara*, whereas the women supplied loose taro corms in garden baskets. In this feast, complete order and control—between the acknowledged leader and his hamlet members, among the households of the hamlet, and between men and women—were indisputably communicated.

The turning of the sod was completed the following month. At that time the members discussed the feast they would hold to mark the successful completion of this important stage in the cultivation process.

> *Copland King*: Next week we shall eat meat. Everyone was afraid of death, but now we have finished seventeen gardens and no one has died. There will be seventeen pots of food for our feast.
>   *Jeremiah*: We were scared of death but now we have triumphed ["triumph" is *vaiuba*, literally "to become cold," which brings to mind its antithesis, magic and sorcery, which are said to be "hot"]. Now we must look for meat. Next week we'll eat well. We'll joke and laugh and be happy. We won't eat rice. We'll eat taro pudding.

When the sod had been turned and a feast marked its completion, the following food was contributed: three pigs (one from Malcolm, one from Jeremiah's sister, and a third one, a wild pig caught by various men from the hamlet), twelve fish (one from nearly every household in the hamlet), three *diwara* (one from Osborne, one from Malcolm's son, and one from a young man), twelve stalks of plantains (one from each male-headed household), and twenty garden baskets of loose taro, breadfruit, yams, and sweet potatoes (one or more basket from each household).

Jeremiah made the decisions about the food distribution, and Osborne carried out the plans by dividing the food into seventeen equal portions. One portion was allotted to each household. Outdoors, each household peeled its food, built its fires, readied its pots, cooked, and ate while remaining separate from the others. Jeremiah thanked everyone for coming and for bringing the food. He asked whether they were happy. They responded that they were. Copland King said, "Today we have food from our land. We have worked together and brought food."

Several differences stand out between this political feast and the one prior to turning the sod. At the earlier feast, only Jeremiah had contributed a pig; this time three pigs were supplied, none by him. Thus the statement about Jeremiah's paramount position within the hamlet made earlier by his contribution of a pig was now minimized. In this latter feast Jeremiah contributed only vegetable food. Second, at the earlier feast, gender categories and male statuses had been deliberately marked by food contributions. Now, in contrast, no such differences were expressed. This time each household supplied plantains as well as garden baskets of loose taro and vegetables. Almost everyone contributed fish. Of the three men who brought *diwara*, two were of low status. Those who provided pork were a rival leader, a woman, and the group as a whole.

Both feasts are political feasts, and each makes a different statement about tensions within the group, about the psychological state of the leader, and about the need for social control. At the first feast, which took place in an atmosphere of anxiety prior to turning the sod, leadership roles were emphasized, gender and status were clearly defined, and male rivalry and hamlet tensions were controlled. The second, which took place after the work was completed when the atmosphere was more relaxed, communicated a lack of regulated leadership as well as the relative equality of gender and of status among male hamlet members.

The differences in the two political messages can be understood within the total context of each feast. The tone of the first was fear ("Men will not fall," "To have three leaders is no good," "Magical substance is in our presence," etc.). The food exchange communicated a tight definition of leadership and social control in anticipation of possible rifts, rivalries, and evil intentions. The second, where the tone was one of elation ("We were scared of death but now we have triumphed," "We shall joke and laugh and be happy," etc.), loosened the controls in retrospective relief.

The need to tighten or relax political control is communicated directly by the use of food at political feasts. Where the political message is one of tension among group members and obedience to one leader, people adhere strictly to the rules of grammar underlying the exchange. When the message is one of fewer tensions, or of the resolution of conflict, the rules of the exchange can be slackened. Such political statements are made symbolically by bundled taro. Who contributes taro and how they do so are actions quickly and unmistakably comprehended by all Wamirans. As one man explained to me, "Taro, not people, are the chiefs at [political] feasts." And, as is true for every successful political activity, organized and effective communication cannot take place without "the chief."

CONCLUSION: IMPLICATIONS FOR DEVELOPMENT

In Wamira, food is exchanged at political feasts in a highly symbolic and carefully coded way. Only bundled taro, with their regenerative stalks attached (symbols of men's virility that hold the power to shame), can be used strategically to increase and manipulate status. Thus when relationships between men are discussed, only taro can speak the appropriate language. In social feasts the messages communicated are less political. Statements are about amiability, solidarity, and cooperation among group members. Any food (other than the symbolically potent political food *diwara*) can be used because it is the sharing of food, not the symbolic value of the food itself, which imparts the message. On such occasions loose taro—or rice—can be used to express social concerns. Taro is such a potent symbol in Wamiran society precisely because it can play both roles. Its multiplicity of functions undoubtedly has contributed to its endurance against the obstacles of an inhospitable environment and, more recently, of introduced changes.

My original question concerned choice between traditional and imported foods. It appears that choice is determined primarily by the type of feast being held and the messages expressed within it. For Wamirans, the decision is rational and is independent of such factors as the availability of money or imported food, factors analyzed by other authors (Bindon 1988; and Sexton 1988). Defying their inhospitable environment, and despite their access to cash and imported foods, Wamirans have chosen to continue their arduous cultivation of taro. They persevere because taro is more than a nutritional morsel. It is a crop with which men identify and to which they attribute an entire range of symbolic and political meaning.

This conclusion about the necessity of exchanging taro during Wamiran political feasts has practical value for planners of development and for policy makers. Food is particularly affected by change in developing Pacific countries. Policy makers are often in the position to mandate different methods of land allocation, to suggest new agricultural technologies, and to introduce cash crops. The complex questions of agricultural change must take into consideration the importance of certain traditional foods for the people concerned. In this instance, developers must consider the sociopolitical role that taro plays in some areas of the Pacific (or yams in other regions) if they are to encourage true independence for developing nations rather than make countries dependent on cash, imported food, and outsiders' (often exploitative) ideas about development.

Encouraging Pacific Islanders to depend upon cash and imported foods may invite more than an economic shift from self-reliance to dependency.

It may simultaneously undermine their sociopolitical systems. If Wamirans were to replace taro with imported foods, for example, they would be stripped of their main symbol of male identity and their primary vehicle for political communication. The replacement of taro with purchased food would force Wamirans to define themselves and their relationships in terms of a symbol—money—devised and controlled by Westerners. Wamirans often have commented to me, "We are taro people, but where you come from people are money people." If a total shift from "taro people" to "money people" were to take place, as some developers might wish, the result would be dependency in *two* realms: the economic and the symbolic. To separate Wamirans from their taro would have effects as far-reaching as ridding Westerners of their money.

NOTES

1. The research upon which this article is based was conducted during two field trips to Wamira, one from June 1976 to March 1978, the other from August 1981 to March 1982. I am very grateful for the generous support of the National Science Foundation, the National Institute of Mental Health, the Wenner-Gren Foundation for Anthropological Research, and the Institute for Intercultural Studies, which made the research financially possible. Those who truly enabled the research to flourish, however, were the Wamirans. I thank those Wamiran friends who patiently and magnanimously helped me with my work, especially the people of Inibuena hamlet who continually included me in their feasts. My deepest gratitude goes to Alice Dobunaba, Aidan Gadiona, and the late Sybil Gisewa for being my family during the two-and-one-half years that I lived with them.
2. In Papua New Guinea, only the Port Moresby area and the Markham Valley suffer from an equivalent lack of rainfall.
3. For specific details on the irrigation system see Kahn 1984.
4. Figures are based on several surveys I conducted at the Dogura trade store in 1977 and 1982.
5. Wamirans do not verbally articulate the fact that there are two different types of feasts. Yet the fact that at each feast the message was further stressed by short speeches indicates that they are conscious of the symbolic content of the food presentations.

REFERENCES

Barth, F. 1966. *Models of Social Organization.* London: Royal Anthropological Institute Occasional Paper, no. 23.
Bell, F. L. S. 1946. "The Place of Food in the Social Life of the Tanga." *Oceania* 17: 139–72.
Bindon, James R. 1988. "Taro or Rice, Plantation or Market: Dietary Choice in American Samoa." *Food and Foodways* 3, 1&2: 59–78.
Buchbinder, G. 1977. "Endemic Cretinism among the Maring: A By-Product of Culture Contact." In T. Fitzgerald, ed., *Nutrition and Anthropology in Action.* Atlantic Highlands, N. J.: Humanities Press, pp. 106–16.
Coyne, T. 1981. *The Effect of Urbanization and Western Diet on the Health of Pacific Island Populations.* Noumea: South Pacific Commission.

Grant, Jill. 1988. "The Effects of New Land Use Patterns on Resources and Food Production in Kilenge, West New Britain." *Food and Foodways* 3, 1&2: 99–117.

Hogbin, I. 1970. "Food Festivals and Politics in Wogeo." *Oceania* 40: 304–28.

Kahn, M. 1983. "Sunday Christians, Monday Sorcerers: Selective Adaptation to Missionization in Wamira." *Journal of Pacific History* 18: 96–112.

―――. 1984. "Taro Irrigation: A Descriptive Account from Wamira, Papua New Guinea." *Oceania* 54: 204–23.

―――. 1986. *Always Hungry, Never Greedy: Food and the Expression of Gender in a Melanesian Society*. Cambridge: Cambridge University Press.

Lea, D. 1969. "Some Non-Nutritive Functions of Food in New Guinea." In F. Gale and G. H. Lawton, eds., *Settlement and Encounter: Geographical Studies Presented to Sir Grenfell Price*. Melbourne: Oxford University Press, pp. 173–84.

Lévi-Strauss, C. 1966. *The Savage Mind*. Chicago: University of Chicago Press.

Meigs, A. S. 1984. *Food, Sex, and Pollution: A New Guinea Religion*. New Brunswick: Rutgers University Press.

Paine, R. 1976. "Two Modes of Exchange and Mediation." In B. Kapferer, ed., *Transaction and Meaning: Directions in the Anthropology of Exchange and Symbolic Behavior*. Philadelphia: Institute for the Study of Human Issues, pp. 63–85.

Parkinson, S. 1982. "Nutrition in the South Pacific—Past and Present." *Journal of Food and Nutrition* 39: 121–25.

Powdermaker, H. 1932. "Feasts in New Ireland: The Social Function of Eating." *American Anthropologist* 34: 236–47.

Sexton, Lorraine. 1988. "'Eating' Money in Highland Papua New Guinea." *Food and Foodways* 3, 1&2: 119–142.

Spriggs, M. 1980. "Taro Irrigation in the Pacific: A Call for More Research." *South Pacific Bulletin* 30: 15–18.

Thaman, R. R. 1982. "Deterioration of Traditional Food Systems, Increasing Malnutrition and Food Dependency in the Pacific Islands." *Journal of Food and Nutrition* 39: 109–121.

Tuzin, D. F. 1972. "Yam Symbolism in the Sepik: An Interpretive Account." *South western Journal of Anthropology* 28: 230–54.

Young, M. W. 1971. *Fighting with Food: Leadership, Values and Social Control in a Massim Society*. Cambridge: Cambridge University Press.

HOSPITALITY, WOMEN, AND
THE EFFICACY OF BEER

Kathryn S. March

The Tamang and the Sherpa are highland Buddhist populations living in Nepal. Both peoples migrated originally from the Tibetan plateau; they share many historical linguistic, religious, social, and cultural roots. The Sherpa have traditionally lived at the highest habitable elevations in the vicinity of Mount Everest in mideastern Nepal; they are renowned as climbers and guides. The Tamang are less well known in the West, even though they are the largest non-Hindu population in Nepal.[1] They live in the hills surrounding the Kathmandu valley from the Buri Gandaki River in the west to the Mt. Everest region in the east.[2]

Sherpa and Tamang social life forms around hospitality. Among their Hindu neighbors, and more widely in South Asia, commensal relations are highly charged. They are marked by their absence in a hierarchy of absences (not touching each other's food, not eating together, not smoking together, etc.), or graduated in a hierarchy of shared and unshared foods (raw but not cooked foods, foods cooked in butter but not those cooked in water, etc.). These Hindu concerns negatively regulate,[3] and generally tend to curtail, mundane hospitality. To Tamang or Sherpa, any such curtailment is the height of effrontery. Not to offer hospitality demonstrates the profoundest social incompetence, and all meaningful interaction among Tamang and Sherpa—whether as simple as that between one-time host and guest or as enduring as that between affines or between people and divinity—is marked by hospitable exchange.

Even casual travelers through Sherpa country concur with Fürer-Haimendorf's observation that "every visit to a Sherpa house is an occasion for the display of an elaborate etiquette" (1964, p. 285). The Sherpa consider it rude, and even dangerous, to allow any guest to leave with an "empty mouth" (see Ortner 1970 and 1978). Sherpa invitations, drink, and food are proffered with a vigor that is ultimately irresistible, although resistance is equally vigorous. All Sherpa exchanges resound with the "Eat! Eat! Eat!" of commensal patrons and the answering "Thank you no! Thank you no! Thank you no!" of their guests. Generous hospitality presses people's resources and sociability to such a degree that at times they choose to avoid one another completely (March 1979).

Hospitality is not so aggressively pursued or resisted among the Tamang, but it dominates their social landscape as well. It is often less elaborate than the Sherpa's, partly but not entirely because the Tamang have more limited means at their disposal. Tamang are frequently apologetic that their hospitality may involve nothing more than a shared cigarette or pipe, but they continue to observe a precise etiquette of hospitable exchange. Guests are expected to be reserved and initially somewhat reluctant, but ultimately they must consume the requisite combinations and numbers of servings. Uninvited guests typically come bearing a modest offering of food and drink; even invited ones often bring something—if only a cigarette—to add to the exchange. Tamang hospitality is, however, decidedly less insistent than that of the Sherpa.

In spite of these stylistic differences, commensal hospitality is extremely common and highly valued in both Sherpa and Tamang communities. All transactions begin with a hospitable offering—of cigarettes,[4] tea, milk, food, and other gifts, but above all of "beer"[5] and "whiskey"—that must be accepted and must be reciprocated. An offering is effective if or because it creates an ambience of amicable feelings.

Tamang and Sherpa versions of hospitality resemble one another in four essential ways: in an assertion of almost perfectly balanced reciprocity; in the ambivalence surrounding the relative social statuses of participants; in the use of hospitality as a model for religious worship; and finally, in the importance of female symbols of mediation in both human and divine hospitality exchanges. This article outlines the first three characteristics only briefly. A more detailed examination of the fourth reinterprets the connections between women, food, fertility, health, and prosperity. Hospitality, which women proffer, induces and reflects those distinctive reciprocal exchanges around which Tamang and Sherpa society forms. At the same time, the underlying female symbolism engenders and expresses profound doubts about the reliability of these exchanges.

SYMMETRICAL EXCHANGE

Unlike the lengthy cycles of asymmetrical complementary exchange that characterize much of the rest of South Asian caste society, Sherpa and Tamang hospitality is predicated upon assumptions of a more nearly immediate and exactly equivalent reciprocity. The model of hospitality followed by both Tamang and Sherpa assumes that the roles of donor and recipient will be reversed over and over again in ongoing cycles of reciprocity.

Among the highly individualistic Sherpa, every exchange motivates not just one but two returns. All hospitality must be "paid for" at the time it is offered, with an answering cup of tea or beer—even if poured from the host's own stocks. Often, repayment is not only immediate but quite literal, as Fürer-Haimendorf observes of a Sherpa mortuary feast: "Those accepting this hospitality placed a few coins on the table where the host was sitting, and such immediate payment for hospitality is considered courteous and in no way detrimental to the host's prestige" (1964, p. 242). Sherpas must also reciprocate with a "return invitation," reckoned in a manner not unlike a diplomatic dinner-party circuit.[6]

Tamang hospitality is less insistent upon immediate individual reciprocity and is strongly colored by the prescription of cross-cousin marriage.[7] Tamang marital exchanges result in cycles that are not as dependent upon individual return, since the exchanges connect not just individuals but whole groups. Nor do they have to be answered immediately, since the social channels along which reciprocity travels can be expected to perdure structurally. But all offers are ultimately matched with a balanced return, and the expectation of eventual balance underlies Tamang exchange just as more immediate return underlies Sherpa exchange. It is rare to find Tamang hospitality exchanges "paid for" in the literal sense found in even casual Sherpa exchanges, except at large mortuary feasts where Tamang ledgers are nonetheless carefully kept and exact contributions are recorded so they can be precisely returned in the future.

EXCHANGE AND HIERARCHY

Within this circular logic—of offerings necessitating repayments, that are themselves construed as offerings necessitating another round of counter-offers—the hierarchy between donor and recipient remains structurally unresolved. At one moment the host/donor is cast as a patron who can afford to give generously. Such generosity is highly valued, especially within the Buddhist conception of meritorious giving. On the other hand, the obligation to receive and the implicit, sometimes even coercive, assumption of a necessary reciprocity suggest to Sherpa and Tamang that the gift is also a request and the donor, in fact, a supplicant.

Sherpa and Tamang men and women engage in hospitality not only to repay their social creditors but also to accrue debtors. Whether they seek help building a house, staging mortuary observances, carrying messages, or arranging a wedding, all Tamang and Sherpa proposals for social cooperation are made within the idiom of offering hospitality. People who want help carry offerings of beer (with or without accompanying snacks) to those whose help they hope to enlist. Through this token hospitality, supplication is recast into generosity that must be reciprocated. Moreover, the donor hopes that people will want to give, that remembered obligations from prior exchanges, as well as the effects of the offered alcohol, will make recipients think fondly of the tie that links them to their host.

Different analyses, especially of the more often studied Sherpa, have interpreted this hospitality in various ways. Fürer-Haimendorf's early studies of Sherpa society focus upon the "warmth and cordiality which pervades the relations between friends and fellow villagers [and] is intensified among close kinsmen, [so that] the atmosphere in the average Sherpa home is one of relaxed and affectionate cheerfulness" (1964, p. 287). His interpretation is consistent with other accounts of Sherpa life as it is experienced within more formalized interactions or on shorter field stays. Such experience of Sherpa society underscores the spirit of amiable cooperation that hospitable interchanges attempt to foster.

Others, including many Sherpa themselves, who have worked and lived in Sherpa communities without the interpersonal cushion provided by trekking organizations, interpreters, professional staffs, or a subsociety of traveling companions, have found the idiom of hospitality at times less merry and more manipulative. Ortner, for example, explores features of Sherpa hospitality that were submerged in Fürer-Haimendorf's work. She pursues what Fürer-Haimendorf only alluded to when he remarked of Sherpa wedding hospitality (see Figure 1), "More and more beer is served, and some of the host's kinsmen are drawn—sometimes dragged—into the circle" (1964, p. 53). Fürer-Haimendorf highlights the many ways in which "the offering and the receiving of hospitality is accompanied by endless courtesies" (1964, p. 244) that "draw" people into social intercourse; Ortner has "dragged" Sherpa "ambivalence concerning hospitality" (1978, p. 64) out of the shadows of his description. Ortner demonstrates how hospitality not only shapes cooperative behavior but is also, sometimes subtly, sometimes sharply, coercive.

Figure 1 Sherpa host entertains wedding guests with copious refills of beer. Although weddings and similar gatherings are occasions for much revelry and enjoyment, they are also the scenes of many violent arguments and physical fights. *Photo: K. S. March.*

Both perspectives recognize that hospitality regulates personal relations and statuses. One asserts that the process "works so smoothly and unobtrusively, that status differences are not unduly emphasized, and there prevails a general atmosphere of equality in which the powerful and the poor mix on easy terms" (Fürer-Haimendorf 1964, p. 286). The other argues that "the core of hospitality lies in the reproduction of that peculiar stringing out of individuals in a minutely graded status hierarchy" (Ortner 1978, p. 83). From this latter vantage point, the impromptu or sudden invitations, the pressuring and protesting, and the joking and jockeying about seating arrangements that characterize Sherpa hospitality are clearly more than just courtesies. They are as much a part of the "almost unremitting play upon the theme of status" (Ortner 1978, p. 84) as are more violent disagreements or fights about individual autonomy and social location, which also typify Sherpa sociality (March 1979, pp. 72–86).

The disparity between Fürer-Haimendorf's and Ortner's interpretations of Sherpa hospitality should not be reduced to a question of ethnographic accuracy. The issue at stake in their divergent representations goes well beyond the Sherpa; it has been central to the theoretical understanding of gift exchanges themselves. Mauss's theory of exchange accords precisely this ambiguity a pivotal importance. "The gift," Sahlins argues in his discussion of Mauss, "affects only will and not right. Thus, the condition of peace as understood by Mauss—and as it in fact exists in the primitive societies—has to differ politically from that envisioned by the classic contract, which is always a structure of submission, and sometimes terror. Except for the honor of generosity, the gift is not sacrifice of equality and never of liberty" (1979, p. 170). Sherpa hospitality exchanges are exemplary of such gift exchanges. They are not regulated by an ideology of hierarchical obligations, although they may ultimately create and display dramatic social and economic asymmetries. Conceptually, however, not "right" but "will," "honor," "generosity," and a panoply of allied sentiments are believed to motivate Sherpa exchanges.

EXCHANGE AND DIVINITY

Sherpa and Tamang obtain social cooperation because givers of hospitality are thought to draw recipients into an obligation to repay that cannot be refused. They convoke the cooperation of divinity in a similar way. Offering rituals invite divinities to become "guests" of their human "hosts."[8] In ritual, divinity is tempted into accepting human hospitality that, because it carries expectations of reciprocity without establishing a clear status hierarchy, involves certain predictable tensions. In Tamang and Sherpa experience of social life, offers of hospitality set a crucial confusion about status, obligation, intimidation, and affection into play. Everyone presumes that the momentum of reciprocal obligation will necessitate repayment, but these exchanges occur in a social framework of idealized equality and generosity which confounds the roles of donor and supplicant. By approaching divinity affines or benefactors, Sherpa and Tamang in their worship try to oblige divine interaction with people to assume the more familiar form of mundane hospitality.

THE PROBLEMATICS OF EXCHANGE

As an exchange between presumptively independent and equal agents, however, this hospitality poses problems. Offerings are gifts that are expected to be returned. The obligation to receive (first highlighted by Mauss 1967, pp. 10–12) operates among Sherpa and Tamang to render refusal structurally irrelevant. An invitation to a Sherpa meal is extended, often by a child barely old enough to express it, after the cooking of the meal is already under way (see also Ortner 1978, p. 80). Guests fortunate enough to have noticed other signals that an invitation was impending can avoid cooking in their own houses. But, more typically, Sherpa invitations arrive as, or after, prospective guests cook and eat in their own houses. Sherpas will try to force even young messengers to accept food before going and then eat again at their hosts' (carrying home what they cannot consume). Even if, under extreme circumstances, they absolutely cannot attend, they must nevertheless repay the unaccepted invitation later. According to Sherpa informants, "Hadn't the hosts' food already been cooked?" Among Tamang villagers, there are many more casual interactions, where invitations can be negotiated, but the imperative to reciprocate remains. In the invitation itself, whether it is accepted, rejected, or passed on to some stand-in, the essential nature of hospitality among both Tamang and Sherpa is transacted.

What makes Tamang and Sherpa exchange most problematic is not that erratic people and divinities might be so uncivilized or hardhearted as to reject an offering—although considerable pressure is sometimes applied to circumvent this recurring frustration—but that the offerings might not behave or be proffered with the spirit proper to evoke a return. At stake in their offerings is the structure of exchange itself. Always they must ask: Are offerings alone sufficient to keep reciprocal exchanges in motion, or does effective exchange depend upon an intrinsic desire for exchange on the part of the items being exchanged or the people exchanging them (or both)?

Mauss's discussion of the Maori concept of *hau* (often inadequately glossed as the "spirit" of a gift) emphasizes that "the spirit of the thing given" is not "inert" (1967, pp. 8–10). The motive or desire to be returned, according to Mauss, is inherent in the idea of the gift itself: "The thing given … is alive and often personified, and strives to bring to its original clan and homeland some equivalent to take its place" (1967, p. 10). Sahlins has since reexamined the materials used by Mauss; he disagrees that any intentionality could reside in the "spirit" of the gift itself (even, or perhaps especially, in the Maori conception of it). Instead, Sahlins argues, hau cannot be interpreted as a soul-like quality inherent in gifts. Rather, it represents the capacity of things exchanged to result in increases: "The 'hau' of a good is its yield, just as the 'hau' of the forest is its productiveness…. The term 'profit' is economically and historically inappropriate to the Maori, but it would have been a better translation than 'spirit'" (1979, pp. 160–61).

Whether it is inherent in the nature of things exchanged to seek return and increased return is what concerns both Tamang and Sherpa as well as Mauss and Sahlins. In many respects, the resonances between these theories of the gift and Sherpa and Tamang ethnography are palpable. At stake is the central question: What guarantees that exchange will result in reciprocal return and, ultimately, the cycles of increasing return that are so desired by those who exchange? Insofar as Tamang and Sherpa exchanges typically involve food, and especially beer, people clearly hope that something in the nature of the things offered will themselves influence the exchange, through ingestion, satiation, and intoxication. In addition, as we shall see, Sherpa and Tamang exchanges do not seek just an adequate reciprocal return; they hope to set in motion great cycles of increase and prosperity. In that respect, then, the significance of the gift is not just its ability to elicit an equal return gift, but the possibility that it will bring profitable returns. In these regards, Mauss and Sahlins have spoken quite eloquently of aspects of the gift that do indeed concern Tamang and Sherpa.

But the Sherpa and Tamang are concerned not only with why exchanges work; they are preoccupied with why too often they do not work. The fabric of their world is woven through such exchanges (March 1984), but it is always precariously near to rupture. When gifts work, when exchange is successful, in these theories of exchange, it operates as if the things exchanged, perhaps, assumed a will to bring returns, in widening circles of profitability. But as Tamang and Sherpa know only too painfully, gifts and exchange do not always work. This makes their awareness that their world depends on the efficacy of exchange poignant indeed. When gifts do not work, could it be because they exercised a will contrary to that of the exchangers? Could it be that, when the possibility of intention is entertained of gifts, a theory is engendered which offers great promise for explaining not only success in exchange but also failure? Here the Sherpa and Tamang evidence most strongly suggests that previous theorists of the gift, like Mauss and Sahlins, have mistakenly placed the emphasis upon what are only possible answers to the gift, thereby ignoring the central cultural focus upon the underlying question itself.

If Tamang and Sherpa hospitality is to be a perfectly reliable mechanism for inducing reciprocal exchange, the offerings themselves must be unmotivated. On the one hand, it would not be acceptable to Sherpa and Tamang if gifts had a "spirit" calling for return, or if they motivated increased returns. For that to occur predictably, however, any will the offerings were to exhibit would have to coincide (or at least not conflict) with the desires of the exchangers. But since it is not in the nature of things with will always to recognize the wills of others, Tamang and Sherpa are caught in the central dilemma of their offerings. Effective though the intentionality of gifts might be in furthering human exchanges, absolutely ideal offerings simply mark enduring and unquestioned exchange, transmitting—like the children who act as messengers on their parents' exchange missions—only the desires of the exchangers but having none of their own to disrupt the system of exchange itself.

WOMEN AND EXCHANGE

It is within this framework that the place of women and the femaleness of exchange unfolds for Tamang and Sherpa. Women and symbols of femaleness are crucial at all levels of exchange—the casual hospitality within villages, the more formal hospitality between affines, and the ritual hospitality of religious practice. It is through ideas about women, hospitality, and especially beer that both women and men think about the desirability of exchange, of mutual obligation and compassion, as well as about the difficulties of sustaining balanced and reliable networks of exchange, especially with divinity.

In general, hospitality is offered by the head woman of the household in her capacity as coparcener[9] of the family's estate and exchange obligations. Her responsibilities are most explicit in formal hospitality and on ritual occasions, when she personally assembles and places offerings (whether or not she cooked them herself) before the honored guests or divinities.[10] (See Figure 2.) The gestures, body movements, and language

Figure 2 Tamang woman places offerings at *Tshe Chhu*, a major communal celebration and dance drama festival. *Photo: K. S. March.*

that accompany the hospitality are highly formalized, and they evoke some of the basic imagery of hospitality for both Sherpa and Tamang.[11] In particular, offerings should be made with the right hand extended, the left hand touching the right elbow, body and head inclined slightly forward. Honorific, even archaic, language should be used. Tamang religious song is explicit about the importance of the "hand of the mistress of the house" and her use of "respectful gestures of invitation" in hospitality exchanges with both people and divinities. The opening lines of a song of creation (the *Ya Hwai*) declare:

> A beautiful mistress of the house,
>   with respectful gestures
>   extends an invitation and says,
>   come sit at ease on this most pleasant of seats.

> A beautiful mistress of the house,
>   extends an invitation and asks,
>   come have something to drink and eat.

The imagery of mistresses in their households, when women engage in such hospitality, converges with that of several female religious figures, notably offering goddesses and mythic female ascetics. All of these female figures are significant in Sherpa and Tamang worship,[12] especially in conceptions of hospitality and mediation as ways of securing divine support and cooperation.

In the widely cited Tibetan Buddhist tradition, the Chhepi Lhamo represent offerings, symbolizing each of the human senses. Each one is pictured iconographically as a beautiful woman in a dancing pose, holding the offering taken to be symbolic of the sensory channel she represents. Tamang and Sherpa specialists recognize six such goddesses: for sight (holding a mirror), sound (a lyre), smell (an incendier), taste, (a *torma* cake), touch (cloth), and thought (a book).

The association between these goddesses and the head woman of a household is especially clear in Sherpa domestic rituals. At the beginning of such rituals the intermediate or "inside" offerings, among which are the Chhepi Lhamo, are placed facing the back of the altar. In monastic performances, iconographic drawings of the Chhepi Lhamo and/or bowls of the offerings they represent operate in a similar manner, to link the human supplicants to divinity and to carry human hospitality offerings to divine "guests." As the ritual progresses and the divinities have been invoked, the senior woman present in a Sherpa household sponsoring the ritual (or her representative),[13] at a signal from the textual officiant, turns the offerings around so that they face forward. This turning marks divine acceptance of the offerings and signals the divine presence in the household altar. The Chhepi Lhamo and the female mediation they represent are indispensable to human efforts at bridging the void between the sensual and profane world, on the one hand, and the limitless domain of divinity, on the other.

Among Tamang the Chhepi Lhamo, although recognized, are somewhat less important to the understanding of ritual than the Bhot Sya, or "Tibetan wife" (*Khangdo Yeshi Chhogya*), and Bai Sya, the "Newar wife" (*Hajam Mandarava*) of the "Guru" (Padmasambhava).[14] These two women were thought to have accompanied the Guru, providing him with food and other creature comforts through his many journeys. Lay people refer to them as his wives; most ritual specialists deny that the Guru was married, saying instead that the Bhot Sya and Bai Sya were *jyomo* or *gelung* (*sya*), "women ascetics" or "monastic (women)" of extraordinary devotion.

Individual people (whether Tamang or Sherpa) tell different stories of the devotion of these women. Having nothing to offer the Guru, according to one account, either because they were poor or because they were ascetics, the Bhot Sya cut off her breast and offered it to him along with her own milk, while the Bai Sya offered water to drink. Another set of stories associates the Bhot Sya's self-mutilation with the origin of meat and blood as tantric[15] religious offerings and the Bai Sya's offering with the tradition of offering fermented "beer" or distilled spirits. In all of the varying tales and in their iconographic representation as the two women flanking the Guru and holding bowls with food and drink out to him, the Bhot Sya and Bai Sya are primarily understood in relation to the offerings they are said to have made to the Guru.[16]

The Chhepi Lhamo (who are more prominent in Sherpa imagery) and the Bhot Sya and Bai Sya (more prominent in Tamang thought) together emphasize the importance of female linkage. They are not, according to the Sherpa and Tamang theory of exchange, "servile." Without the intercession of the Chhepi Lhamo, or of Bhot Sya and Bai Sya, human offerings would be utterly ineffectual. These female figures are often referred to in the Buddhological literature as "lesser" or "minor" divinities, or as subordinate supplicants themselves only one step "higher" than the human worshippers they represent. But the very ambiguity about status, rank, and the nature of the exchange relation in the Tamang and Sherpa contexts precludes such unequivocal devaluation. Sherpa and Tamang offerings are not simple prestations, marking a social or religious hierarchy; rather, they evoke a relation of precarious balance—between unmotivated meritorious generosity, on the one hand, and manipulative, even coercive, self-interest, on the other. The Chhepi Lhamo, Bhot Sya, and Bai Sya are necessarily partners in this Tamang and Sherpa conception of reciprocal exchange, not handmaidens to that different view of asymmetrical exchange reportedly found in other parts of South Asia.

The idea of obligating divinity into exchanging with humanity through hospitality does not, of course, carry equal value in all contexts. Inasmuch as convivial inducements are sensual, while the ultimate objectives of orthodox Buddhist pursuits are spiritual, hospitality operates in a devalued domain. But religious pursuits are not always, nor for everyone, exclusively spiritual. In the Buddhism familiar to both Sherpa and Tamang the relation is never resolved between the desire for worldly blessings, which include wealth, health, and power, and the striving for an otherworldly sensibility that denies the ultimate reality of the human world. When the primary religious objective is to remove oneself entirely from the mundane and sensual world, hospitality itself represents one of the bonds to a false world which must be broken. But Tamang and Sherpa ritual, by its use of the hospitality model, focuses as much upon the "downward" or reciprocal movement of blessings from divinity to humanity as it does upon the intended "upward" or renunciatory movement of Buddhist human worship. (See Figure 3.) Thus worship not only attracts or propitiates divinity, thereby mediating human attempts to reach the divine, but also motivates a return exchange or blessing.

It is not surprising to find Sherpa and Tamang women, in their identification with female religious figures of hospitality, behaving like confident hostesses. They enter into social exchanges with none of the coquetry, hesitancy, or modesty that might betoken subordination. Indeed, both Sherpa and Tamang women are lively hostesses, entertaining guests with striking candor, liberally offering drink and the snacks that accompany it, and at the same time consciously engaging in carefully constructed exchanges. As Fürer-Haimendorf observed, "while Sherpas are very free in verbal expressions and a male visitor may joke with his hostess in a manner which in many other societies would be considered outrageous, both hostess and visitor will seldom fail to maintain the strictest etiquette in the serving and acceptance of drink" (1964, p. 285).

Such behavior is, I contend, consistent with the shared Tamang and Sherpa view of reciprocity, hospitality, and women; these ideas center around the place of beer. As Sherpa and Tamang women entertain their guests, and especially as they proffer beer, they self-consciously attempt to recreate the ambience—ideally of loving generosity, but failing that, at least of responsible and courteous reciprocity—within which they believe the human world was framed.

Figure 3 Mistress of a Sherpa household receives a blessing on her forehead from the local lama after the "inside" offerings have been turned around, indicating the arrival of divine presence (and, it is hoped, blessings) in the house. *Photo: K. S. March.*

It is through the "hand of the mistress of the house" that social life comes into being and that the reciprocal blessings of divinity come into the household. This aspect of female mediation is most explicit in Tamang blessing rituals. The head woman of the household receives a blessing for health, fertility, and general prosperity, not just for herself but as a representative for her entire household. (See Figure 4.) The woman is seen as the channel not only for communicating offerings "up" to divinity but also for receiving the hoped-for reciprocal blessings back "down" again. It is through the "hand of the mistress" that the Tamang hope to get from divinity their many blessing: *nhor-ki yang*, "fortune" (literally "wealth of increase/prosperity"), *bru-i hong*, "prolific harvests" (literally "grain-of increase/prosperity"), *Khatang she*, "food" (literally "mouth-for things"), *lha-la nhor*, "wealth" (literally, "hand of wealth"), and *chhalam bulam*, "sons" and "daughters," as well as keeping at bay a variety of such undesirable disruptions as illness and gossip. Women in Sherpa ritual, too, are more closely associated with the "good fortune" and health of their families and herds than are their husbands. Both Tamang and Sherpa women monitor what they eat or otherwise expose themselves to more carefully than do men, in a conscious attempt not only to maintain their own physical and spiritual well-being but also to guard against the entrance of impurities into their families.

The importance of female mediation in hospitality exchanges, especially as exchanges provide a vehicle by which health and prosperity enter human households, is clearest in the imagery surrounding beer. Only women, and above all the head woman in each household, make the yeast for brewing, brew beer, and distill the stronger liquors. Women are also closely associated with the serving of these drinks, especially when they are offered on formal social or ritual occasions. At all stages of production and serving, yeast and beer are surrounded by mythology and rituals that display the intricate female symbolism of exchange.

One of the most beautiful traditional Tamang songs is the *Brama-i namtar*, "the tale (or history) of the beer-yeast." Initially the song provides a series of instructions about the proper ingredients and treatments to ensure that yeast will make beer tasty and strong; then it gives instructions for the proper ways in which to offer such drink in hospitality, especially divine hospitality, so as to obtain the desired cooperation and blessings. This song is one of the most powerful known among the Tamang; it cannot be sung casually, since its very singing is to confer the blessings it describes. (See Figure 5.) In particular, it is sung, in a secretive ritual performed behind the closed doors of houses where no children have been born, to cure infertility, bringing a most explicit "increase and prosperity."

Figure 4 Tamang woman receives a blessing from a shaman, holding a glass of beer. Such blessings can be given on pilgrimage, as is the case here, or kneeling before her "life force tree" in front of her house after night-long shamanic rituals. *Photo: K. S. March.*

Figure 5 A Tamang lama prepares the offerings required before the singer can sing, even for the anthropologists, the song about the creation of the beer and butter yeast. Note the butter pats adorning the lip of the traditional beer jug on his right. *Photo: D. H. Holmberg.*

In Sherpa communities, too, women make yeast and beer; there also these activities are vividly colored with the imagery of increased and plenty, although the connotations of human fertility are less explicit than among the Tamang.

In this Tamang song, as in many other contexts both Sherpa and Tamang, an elaborate mythology surrounds yeast, brewing, and beer-offerings. Women are associated not only with the production of beer but also with the many blessings—of health, strength, fertility, prosperity, plenitude, and general increase—that fermented and distilled offerings are thought to secure. For both the Sherpa and Tamang, beer is food in the process of increasing. The aspiration underlying offerings of beer is that the natural propensity of yeast and beer to multiply, heat up, froth, and bubble will spill over into an analogous growth and prosperity for those placing the offerings. For the Sherpa, this imagery remains generalized, touching upon household, farm, herds, and the community as a whole. Among the Tamang, it acquires an additional specific: human fertility and fecundity. In both Tamang and Sherpa imagination, as yeast multiplies and culminates in the most social and sacred of foods (the most efficacious of offerings), so the mistress of the house is responsible for increasing the hospitable and mutually supportive interactions both among people and between people and divinities. She thereby promotes the overall growth and prosperity of her household (see also Ortner 1972).

The most elaborate contexts for offering beer to promote increase are *kyeka* (both Tamang and Sherpa term), *karsyol* (term found only among Tamang), and *yangdzi* (term only among Sherpa). All involve the respectful offering of beer, almost always accompanied by valued and especially tasty foods. Properly speaking, kyeka is exchanged between affines and operates similarly among Sherpa and Tamang, although some of the prestige foods that accompany the kyeka differ, as does the frequency of the offerings. Karsyol and yangdzi are associated with the opening exchanges of religious ritual, but they also apply to a very wide range of hospitality offerings, from impromptu requests for a favor to complex arrangements of ritual offerings.[17] In all these beer-offerings, drink is offered in the most prestigious and respectful manner possible, with careful hand and body gestures, proper offering phrases, and with three small pats of butter or pinches of flour spaced around the rim of the offering cup or jug. No major social or religious event can transpire without an offering along the lines of kyeka, karsyol, or yangdzi. (See Figure 6.)

It is around beer, and especially the beer-offerings of kyeka, karsyol, and yangdzi, that the special implications of the female symbolism of Tamang and Sherpa hospitality emerge. "The reason for the *Brama-i namtar* is to

Figure 6 Tamang woman shaman photographed at her request, in a pose she entitled "bringing *kyeka*." She holds a traditional beer jug respectfully in her hands. *Photo: K. S. March.*

explain the meaning of the karsyol," I was told by a Tamang ritual specialist, although I had asked why it was sung to cure infertility.

> Just as we have made the distilled liquor offering in the karsyol, so we want divinity
> to make a child. So we place karsyol offerings before the divinities asking their aid in
> this respectful way.
>
> Now, this is the reason that the placing of the karsyol is woman's work. Men do not
> do karsyol. If a man must send the offering and there is no woman in his household to
> do it, rather than do it himself, he will find some woman, any woman, from his village
> and ask her to do it for him.
>
> This is the work that suits [is proper to] women. Women make the beer and distill
> the liquor. Women make the liquor offerings.

This specialist was talking in somewhat extravagant terms about the connection between women, beer-making, fertility, and karsyol-offerings
among the Tamang. Nevertheless, there is a logic to the efficacy of beer
offerings shared by Sherpa and Tamang: as yeast increases, so beer is
exchanged to promote general-material increase (food, goods, herds,
wealth) as part of a system of social increase through the reproduction and
expansion of marital exchange and, among the Tamang at least, sexual
reproduction as well. Symbols of femaleness conceptually unite these forms
of increase and plenitude for both Tamang and Sherpa: yeast is thought to
mate to reproduce as do women, and so beer is properly offered in exchange
by women; similarly, the social and marital exchanges through which
Tamang and Sherpa society perdures and prospers are seen as the special
province of women. Prosperity results from the movement of women and
maintenance of ties by and through women. And it is women who have special responsibilities not only to bear and care for children but also to manage and foster the material prosperity of their marital households.

FEMALENESS AND RUPTURE

A clear understanding of the female symbolism of mediation found in
Tamang and Sherpa hospitality exchanges, and especially in these beer-
offerings, has implications for our understanding of female symbolism in
many other contexts. Conceptually, I find it useful to organize these implications into three general categories: first, to embed hospitality firmly
within the specific view of exchange at play among Sherpa and Tamang;
second, to approach the femaleness of hospitality and its benefits as culturally specific symbols; and finally, to explore the place of affect in these
female symbols.

In Tamang and Sherpa society and belief, as we have seen, apparently familiar ideas[18] about women, food and drink, hospitality, fertility, and prosperity, reveal upon closer inspection a very different array of associations. Sherpa and Tamang exchange pivots upon a balanced reciprocity, whether compassionate or coerced, between presumptive equals. This daily domestic hospitality also informs even the most sacred exchanges. As a result, I have cautioned against interpreting generous hostesses as "servile." Instead, their actions perform culturally significant mediations between the mundane world of family life and the bounty of the divine domain. When exchange itself is wealth, when reciprocal obligation secures all that is desirable, and when even divine generosity can be motivated by the irresistibility of hospitality mediated by female symbols, offering—as imagery and as act—is extremely powerful.

Beer-offerings to divinity constitute a sacred hospitality, an effort to perpetuate bonds of reciprocal obligation between the human and divine worlds much as they serve to reinforce such ties in everyday reality as perceived by Tamang and Sherpa. It thus seems apparent, especially in the imagery surrounding beer-offerings, that female mediation is the avenue along which divine bounty might be cajoled back into human life. Beer-offerings bring divine concern, beneficence, compassion, and quite specifically, extra riches, wealth, harvest, health, and prosperity, directly into human life.

The fertility that women's ritual hospitality brings into their households must, however, be placed in its wider cultural context. It is not a simple biological fecundity; in fact, human reproduction and sexuality attract modest attention. Instead, the imagery of beer yeast, as well as beer-offering, emphasizes that the "fertility" gained by women's sacred hospitality is best conceived as "increase," a *general* multiplication of fortune, goods, and in this context children, harvests, and herds.

But there is more to the "tale of yeast" and the story of beer-offerings. The "femaleness" of these offerings draws our attention not only to the fundamental aspirations of the Tamang and Sherpa model of hospitality but also, and perhaps most importantly, to the central ambiguity within their theory of exchange. The question of whether Sherpa and Tamang exchange is a mutually satisfactory and predictable reciprocity, or a fundamentally precarious system of coercion (as if it could be either one or the other) is not one to be answered through ethnographic precision. Such a question in fact masks a crucial observation: mutuality and coercion, balance and bribery, affection and self-interest, all coexist at the very heart of Tamang and Sherpa exchange. In this context, female symbols revolve around fundamentally contradictory, but intimately interconnected, assertions (see also March 1980): that women are, and are not, themselves objects of exchange; that women are, and are not, giving expression to their own desires in exchanges of their own.

When these pairs of interlaced contradictions themselves interact—in the femaleness of sacred hospitality—they constitute the framework within which Sherpa and Tamang are moved both to consider the efficacy of their exchange model and to confront its weaknesses. Sahlins's lengthy comparison of Mauss and Hobbes (1979, pp. 149–83) revolves around these two authors' "similar appreciation of reciprocity as the primitive mode of peace" (p. 178). Reciprocity and exchange are seen as representing a generalized primitive means of reducing social conflict, if not precisely a social contract for community. But social disruption appears equally imminent to Hobbes, Mauss, Sahlins, Sherpa, and Tamang. All require a further explanation for the persistence of people's commitment to sociality and exchange. Sherpa and Tamang ponder this paradox in the femaleness of exchange. Female symbols highlight the simultaneous desirability of guaranteed returns, including divine liberality, and its impossibility.

Two female religious figures, Gang Jyungmo among Tamang and Gelungma Palmo among Sherpa, are vital to this more intricate interpretation of the female symbolism of sacred hospitality. The stories of these two great ascetics are quite long and vary in many respects, but they share certain threads of interest to the argument of this article. Both are presumed to have been historical figures, women who wanted to pursue a religious life, and both underwent great trials in their efforts to achieve spiritual enlightenment and recognition.

Gelungma Palmo suffered disease, humiliation, and challenge—even from her own father, who accused her of having contracted venereal disease—before her spiritual worth was realized.[19] There are several versions of her story; they diverge on at least one significant point. In some of the tellings, especially the more orthodox or monastic ones, Gelungma Palmo's illnesses were cured when she finally learned to devote herself absolutely to Chenrezig (Avalokitesvara).[20] In other renderings she accumulated the requisite power not only to cure herself but to cut off her own head, fly into the air to dance as a headless body, and then descend and reattach her head herself.

In all accounts she is associated with the establishment of the foremost ritual of self-sacrifice, atonement, and meritorious giving practiced in Sherpa regions, the ritual of Ngyunge. According to most lay informants, the ritual is addressed to Gelungma Palmo, who "discovered" the texts and rites that today constitute the event; according to more literate specialists,

Chenrezig is the primary object of attention in Ngyunge and Gelungma Palmo was exemplary in his worship. In both lay and learned exegesis, however, the contradictory objective of Ngyunge is to achieve perfect detachment from all worldly ties while convincing Chenrezig/Gelungma Palmo to provide protection and blessings. The fasting, prostrations, and prayers explicitly attempt to get people to recognize the futility of, and loose themselves from, the entire network of reciprocal obligations that constitutes normal domestic life.[21] But many, if not all, participants in Ngyunge also seek material benefit and physical well-being through the intercessionary compassion of Chenrezig/Gelungma Palmo, a compassion they presume that their self-effacing generosity will necessitate.

Some of Gang Jyungmo's story among the Tamang parallels that of Gelungma Palmo among the Sherpa. Gang Jyungmo, too, studied and worked to become an ascetic and monastic. Her efforts, too, led her into circumstances that brought her religious devotion into question and, temporarily at least, brought her near to ignominy. In her case, however, it was not venereal illness but pregnancy that caused scandal. She claimed to have become pregnant by swallowing a hailstone, but no one would believe her; she was turned out of the monastery and reviled. She is thought eventually to have redeemed herself; today she is regarded by western Tamang both as the founder of Boudha, one of the largest pilgrimage places in Nepal, and as the originator of the practice of fermenting and offering beer in both social and ritual exchanges of hospitality. She is now considered an incarnation of Chenrezig, specifically embodying his compassionate generosity.

Both Gelungma Palmo and Gang Jyungmo are considered models of selflessness, whose generosity and tolerance for adversity surpassed even the most demanding Tamang and Sherpa social models. They are credited with teaching people not only how to imitate the detachment of divine compassion (embodied, in more orthodox interpretations, in Chenrezig) but also how to oblige that divine compassion to remember human vulnerability to illness, hunger, and abandonment. In myth, song, and ritual the full returns of reciprocity (whether compassionate or coerced) emerge as Gelungma Palmo and Gang Jyungmo are considered.

For this analysis of the femaleness of hospitality, however, the special difficulties that the two female ascetics faced in getting recognition for their true spiritual worth are particularly important. Both female figures developed within what can only be termed religious crisis. Gelungma Palmo could not convince people that her various illnesses were signs of spiritual trial, not impurity or vile living; Gang Jyungmo's claim that her pregnancy was supernaturally caused was similarly doubted. Presumably, both Gelungma Palmo and Gang Jyungmo had their own doubts at times (or at least so informants say in telling their stories). At the very least, it is certain that these two female figures and the ritual complexes that originate with them provide a crucial context for Sherpa and Tamang to confront the possibility that reciprocal exchange, especially with divinity, cannot be guaranteed.

The problem is less a matter of determining whether divinities or people are compassionate or self-centered, or whether exchange is freely given or coerced, than the more unsettling consideration that hospitality does not work to bind people (and divinities) together at all. Offerings cannot acquire any will, intention, or desire of their own if the exchange is to proceed without complication. If hospitality offerings are not guileless markers that simply connect the elements in a superordinate system of exchange but instead are themselves considered elements capable of intentions, then the essential reliability of exchange, as Sherpa and Tamang conceive of it, is called into question.

Here the special femaleness of Tamang and Sherpa offerings comes into play. The exchange that female symbols engender is only hypothetically unmotivated. Ideas about women, hospitality, and exchange are embedded in the much wider framework of women and marriage. In that framework the question for the Sherpa and Tamang, as for many contemporary anthropologists, is precisely whether women can be considered simple objects of exchange or whether they might not have desires of their own (Baal 1975). The possibility that women and symbols of femaleness might be motivated in part by purposes of their own threatens the transparency of exchange. The analogous debate within anthropology generally tries either to defend the superordinate nature of exchange—thus objectifying women—or to demonstrate that women maneuver their socially defined egos with the same fundamental self-awareness of men. The female symbolism of Tamang and Sherpa exchange underscores *both* facets in all human relations. The offerings one proffers to induce a return are female, but femaleness is ambiguous: its nature is both to connect and to rupture.

FEMALENESS AND AFFECT

Sherpa and Tamang belief confronts this ambiguity in female symbolism through an exploration of the place of affect in those symbols. The efficacy of exchange does not depend only, or even primarily, upon the question of whether gift offerings themselves desire a return. Rather, it depends on whether givers and receivers are of a "heart and mind" (Sherpa and

Tamang *sem*) to keep up the effort successfully. Sahlins notes that both Hobbes and Mauss turn to human reason as the basis for a commitment to the primitive peace instituted by exchange—their "similar appreciation of reciprocity as the primitive mode of peace; and also, if this more marked in Hobbes than in Mauss, a common respect for the rationality of the undertaking." But Sahlins reports that this "common respect" is somewhat uneasy in both Hobbes and Mauss: "neither Mauss nor Hobbes could trust in the efficacy of reason alone" (1979, p. 178). "Mauss ... concentrated singularly on the anthropomorphic qualities of the things exchanged" (p. 180), and Sahlins wants us to reconsider, without "the Anglo-American reaction of distrust" (1979, p. 181), "the (thinglike?) qualities of the people" (p. 180), "the commercialization of persons apparently implied in the Maussian formula" (Sahlins 1979, p. 181). I want to demonstrate how Sherpa and Tamang belief accomplishes this complex task, through its contemplation of affect in hospitable offerings—a contemplation carried on through female symbolism.

By their imputed femaleness, offerings acquire a potential for independent will, intentions, and desires. Although always structurally significant as simple links, without independent motivation, the symbols of female mediation must ultimately be considered as active intermediaries, capable—like women in marriage, hospitality, and other interpersonal exchange network—of either facilitating exchange or undermining it, depending upon how they feel about it. When women themselves desire exchange, when female offerings are motivated by the presumed cooperation, supportiveness, selflessness, and generosity of women, then, and only then, is exchange assured. Offerings, because of their femaleness, cannot—by the Sherpa and Tamang at least—be construed as without intention, but if offerings do not adopt the desires of the exchangers as their own, exchange is precarious indeed. These possibilities, interpreted through the femaleness of offerings, introduce a crucial tension, including the danger of failure, into the Tamang and Sherpa theory of exchange as it unfolds in both daily and ritual life.

Symbols of female mediation do not simply serve up hospitality offerings; their personal compassion and engagement in the exchange is the only guarantee of its efficacy. The patterns for entertaining and pleasing guests, described in the creation song cited above, are associated not only with the proper performance of the gestures of hospitality but also with the attentive concern and "affection" of women.

> The affection and compassion
> in the hearts and minds
> of our beloved women is great.

> Extending invitations and saying,
>   with the affection and compassion
>   of their hands,
>   come sit at ease on this most pleasant of seats.
>
> Extending invitations and saying,
>   with the affection and compassion
>   of their hearts and minds,
>   come sit at ease on this most pleasant of seats.

In this song the "affection and compassion" of the "hands" as well as the "hearts and minds" of "beloved women," "beautiful mistresses of their houses," are what bring into being all the other elements of the song and, ostensibly, the entire universe—the sky, the earth, time, domestic and social life, colors, birds, plants .... In short, after their respectful offerings, presented both with the external signs of care (the gestures of their "hands") and with an internal identification (in their "hearts and minds"), everything else came into being, "wandered and filled the world," and eventually "faded away and died."

A similar emphasis upon women's affection as the basis for effective, generous reciprocity emerges in the beer-making song (see Appendix for full text).

> As it was in the beginning, let's make good beer.
> When the affection of the women, our beloved daughters, is great
> with their own hands they respectfully offer both food and drink.
> When inviting with the karsyol beer-offering
>   marked with pure unclarified butter,
> do make the beer well.
> It's the blessing of the Guru;
>   it's the blessing of power and strength of life.
> As it was in the beginning, let's make good beer.
> It's the blessing of the Guru;
>   it's the blessing of power and strength of life.

Two recurrent phases in the song—"when the affection of the women, our beloved daughters, is great," and "it is the blessing of the Guru, it is the blessing of the power and strength of life"[22]—highlight the perceived importance of women's love in securing the most general of all the blessings obtained by beer-offerings.

When "the affection of women is great," they might carry offerings with compassion. When the beer is sweet and strong, "as it was in the beginning," it might succeed in obliging even divine generosity. But under all the confidence in this peculiarly (if not uniquely) Sherpa and Tamang view of a necessary reciprocity between equals, lurk doubts. Framed by female symbols is the possibility that other people and divinities, like women— when they act not in their capacity as markers of mediation but as ordi- nary, ambiguously self-serving people—might be either too removed or too narcissistic to care about others' human needs. Under such conditions even the most seductive of offerings might not induce persons or divinities to admit to the bonds of obligation.

NOTES

I am grateful for overall support of my work in Nepal from the National Institute of Mental Health in 1975–77 and from Cornell University in 1982. For comments and criticism, I am most specifically in the debt of Michael Allen, Sherry Ortner, and James Siegel. As always, it is impossible for me to write of Nepal without acknowledging my basic gratitude to David Holmberg.

1. The Nepal census does not collect information on ethnicity, but according to the 1971 Nepal census figures on "Mother Tongue," out of a total national population of 11,555,983 there were 555,056 (or 4.8%) reported speakers of "Tamang." Of these, 8,467 are reported in districts outside traditional areas of Tamang residence, notably 3,867 in Dhaulagiri and 4,198 in Karnali; these latter "Tamang" speakers would probably be iden- tified not as Tamang but as Thakali by contemporary ethnologists. Holmberg (1980) also argues that, due to the relatively low perceived status of being identified as "Tamang," overall figures underrepresent the Tamang presence in Nepal; he suggests that, even excluding the problems of Tamang-Thakali identification in the far west, the Tamang pop- ulation is probably closer to 5–6% of the total Nepalese population. Because the 1971 census did not disaggregate "Sherpa" speakers from speakers of other Tibetan dialects in Nepal, it is also somewhat difficult to estimate the Sherpa population accurately. According to the 1971 census, there were 79,218 (or 0.7% of the total population) speak- ers of "Bhote-Sherpa" in the whole country. Of these, 32,795 are reported well outside traditional areas of Sherpa residence; they probably represent other Tibetan-language speakers. In the regions of predicted Sherpa residence, there were 46,423 (or 0.4% of the total) reported speakers of "Bhote-Sherpa"; this is probably a more realistic estimate.

2. There are historical complexities in the emergence of the Tamang as an ethnic group in modern Nepal, which cannot be addressed here (see Holmberg 1980). In this article, all references to the "Sherpa" and "Tamang" refer exclusively to the Sherpa in the southern (Solu) ranges of the Everest region and the Tamang of the Rasuwa/Nuwakot region north and west of Kathmandu.

3. Except, of course, in the obligations to give to Brahmins.

4. More common among Tamang than Sherpa, many of whom find smoke esthetically and religiously offensive.

5. Hereafter I gloss all the various fermented beverages ("beers") and the distilled one ("whiskey") simply as "beer," although all kinds figure in the exchanges I describe. I do so, in large part, because all these kinds of alcoholic drink are typically referred to in myth and song as "beer" by Sherpa and Tamang themselves.

6. The relative familiarity of these exchanges to Westerners is, I believe, one of the major factors behind the popularity of trekking in Sherpa Nepal.

7. In another study I explored the connections between Tamang and Sherpa conceptions of femaleness and the social position of women in systems of marital exchange (March 1979; 1980). In the consideration of hospitality exchanges there, I give more attention to the impact of models of reciprocity between affines.

8. This, of course, is one of the "key" metaphors of Ortner's entire thesis (1970), and is one of the pivotal ones to which she has returned in her most recent book (1978, see especially pp. 141–56).

9. Tamang and Sherpa women are more active partners of their men than is the case among many other Nepalese and South Asian groups. They inherit, own, and control important property. Moreover, women work actively in household and field production, and they share domestic and childcare duties with their husbands more nearly equally than in most other South Asian communities. It is for this reason, as well as the arguments about exchange specific to this article, that Sherpa and Tamang women can appropriately be called "coparceners," partners or joint heirs.

10. Except, of course, where ritual offerings are the province of a ritual specialist, but even when specialists are called in, they typically work most closely with the woman of the house.

11. Indeed, elsewhere (1979) I have argued that this imagery is so highly stylized that, although it is unquestionably female, it can be evoked in the behaviors of both men and women.

12. For a more detailed discussion of all of these female religious figures, see March 1979.

13. Among Sherpas, often a village lama.

14. Called "Guru Pema" in everyday Tamang, and "Guru Rimpoche" in Sherpa, he was the founder of Tibetan Buddhism and is the central "saint" of Tamang and Sherpa Buddhism.

15. Originally, the Buddhism of the historical Buddha taught that devotees should learn to live without desires for material pleasure in order to obtain release from the mundane world of repeated rebirths. Both Tamang and Sherpa practice Mahayana Buddhism: the Sherpa have historically been associated with the oldest, or "Red Hat" Nyingmapa sects, although recent immigrations of Gelugpa, or "Yellow Hat," monastics are effecting major changes; when orthodoxy has reached Tamang in the Rasuwa/Nuwakot regions to the north and west of Kathmandu, it appears historically to display Dukpa, or Bhutanese, influences. Although there are important differences following the sectarian history of Buddhism, Mahayana Buddhist practice among Sherpa and Tamang is heavily influenced by the disavowal of a split between the material this-world of sensory attractions and a spiritual otherworld without rebirth. Tantric practices in Mahayana tradition encourage devotees to seek precisely those experiences otherwise prescribed, to engage in explicitly sensual pleasures—sex, food, and drink—ostensibly to force them to overcome the "false dualisms" between a material and spiritual world emphasized by earlier ascetic (even if moderatedly ascetic) Buddhisms. Sex, of course, was precluded in the celibacy exacted of orthodox Buddhist devotees of all sects. Food was supposed to be regarded as a necessary bodily fuel but not to be indulged; gluttony, including especially the eating of meat or the drinking of blood, of course, necessitated violating the Buddhist stricture against killing. In many ways, however, it is the tantric indulgence in alcohol that is seen most to violate early Buddhist orthodoxy. A popular religious parable tells of a man given the choice between having sex with a woman, killing a goat to eat, or drinking beer. He chose the beer, thinking it the least of these evils, but, after drinking the beer, got drunk, raped the woman, and slaughtered the goat anyway.

16. In general, contemporary Sherpa religious thought is rationalizing away from tantric indulgences and interpretation; Tamang practice still embraces animal sacrifice, although not by lamas. Among contemporary Tamang, the two women are associated with the beer and other desirable food offerings (including meat), while among the Sherpa their offerings are just as hospitable but today involve meat less frequently. In both cases, their offerings are at the heart of hospitable exchange.

17. For more on yangdzi, see both Fürer-Haimendorf 1964 and Ortner 1978.

18. A crucial issue in considering cross-cultural sexual symbolism pivots on distinguishing those points at which similarities appear to translate across cultures from those at which they do not. This has both trivial and nontrivial consequences. In this article, for example, regardless of apparent Western predilections for perceiving beer imagery as (according to

one reviewer) "a rather good male symbol as it froths and bubbles over," the question is not whether beer (or anything else) *could* be a productive symbolic vehicle for cultural ideas about sex or gender but, rather, whether in the context under consideration it is *perceived* that way. Tamang and Sherpa perceptions of women, beer, hospitality, and increase, then, are in some ways reminiscent of our own but ultimately, because they draw upon a very different system of marriage and society, as well as different cultural and religious abstractions of gender, differ profoundly. The focus of this essay is not, however, the structure of Tamang or Sherpa gender beliefs but the location of affect at the intersection of the place of women as social actors and of femaleness as gender symbol.

19. According to Sherpa belief, disease itself marks spiritual impurity.

20. Chenrezig is a central figure in Tibetan Buddhism. Thought to have achieved enlightenment but rejected Nirvana, Chenrezig remains engaged in the ordinary world, out of "compassion," in order to assist the enlightenment of others.

21. See Ortner's more elaborate description of why this contradiction in Ngyunge is especially pertinent to older Sherpas (1978).

22. For the Tamang, the phrase *Guru Tshe-ki Wang* does not name a Guru, like Guru Pema, but itself represents the most expansive of all blessings, known in other contexts (where imperatives of musical meter do not apply) simply as *tshe-wang* ("the blessing of the power and strength of life," sometimes referred to as the "long-life blessing"). The phrase here implicitly associates the Guru with the "blessing of the power and strength of life," and with beer. For the Sherpa, the Guru's connection with beer and the blessings of beer are more explicit, since he is credited in their accounts with the invention of beer.

APPENDIX

Brama-I Namtar

("The Tale of the Beer Yeast")

This version of "The Tale of the Beer Yeast" was sung by a prominent *shyeponpo*, or "song specialist," on 26 September 1976 in the Karki Mana Kamana region of north-central Nepal. In order to tape the song, ritual offerings of beer, incense, and grains had to be placed and the house closed to outsiders. It is perhaps not coincidental that there was a severe thunderstorm raging outside on the night that the shyeponpo volunteered to sing for the recording since that, too, reduced the chances of the song being overheard. The translation is my own. Proper names of many divinities are not translated; similarly, some plant species and other referents beyond my abilities in Tamang remain in the original. Because of the importance of this song in Tamang belief, the original Tamang language is not reproduced in its entirety, but it can be made available on special request to the author.

(1)
As it was in the beginning,
    at the time of first coming to rebirths,
    let's make good beer;

do make the beer well!
With the water, the water of Lhasa, that we may drink,
with the rice, the rice of the Newars,
—as it was in the beginning, let's make good beer—
with the rice, the rice of the Newars!
(2)
As it was in the beginning, let's make good beer;
do make the beer well.
Take the yeast made from all the right herbs,
—let's make good beer—
and moisten it with the water.
As it was in the beginning, let's make good beer!
(3)
As it was in the beginning, let's make good beer;
do make the beer well.
With the male-and-female of the husking pounder,
let's make good beer,
With lots and lots of grain in the cavity beneath the husking pounder,
As it was in the beginning, let's make good beer.
Fill the hollow beneath the husking pounder full!
(4)
As it was in the beginning, let's make good beer;
Sprinkle flour over the surface of the yeast cakes.
Let's make good beer; do make the beer well.
There's the divinity of the birthing places.
As it was in the beginning, let's make good beer.
There's the divinity of the birthing places.
(5)
As it was in the beginning, let's make good beer;
do make the beer well.
Let it be the hand of the mistress of the house,
—let's make good beer—
that touches and sees if the yeast has gotten warm!
As it was in the beginning, let's make good beer;
Touch and see if the yeast has gotten warm.
(6)
As it was in the beginning, let's make good beer;
do make the beer well.
Let it please the women, our beloved daughters,
      whose hearts and minds are filled with a great affection,
let's make good beer; do make the beer well.

It's the blessing of the Guru;
> it's the blessing of power and strength of life.

(7)
As it was in the beginning, let's make good beer;
do make the beer well.
Let the yeast be mixed with the mash.
Let's make good beer;
Take and wrap it with the leaf of the "pamu parlu" tree.
As it was in the beginning, let's make good beer.
Take the leaf of the "pamu parlu" tree!

(8)
As it was in the beginning, let's make good beer.
Let the beer be strong enough that we might stagger some from it.
Do make the beer well.
Oh! But beer tastes so good!
As it was in the beginning, let's make good beer.
Oh! But beer tastes so good!

(9)
As it was in the beginning, let's make good beer;
do make the beer well.
When inviting the Vajra Guru to come sit at the top,
—let's make good beer—
saying, "Please come inside, please sit in 'urken'!"
As it was in the beginning, let's make good beer.
"Please come inside, please sit in 'urken.' "

(10)
As it was in the beginning, let's make good beer.
Let the mouth be not empty.
Let the hand be not empty,
by hand have I placed these precious offerings
> (for casting a horoscope).

Let's make good beer.
It's the blessing of the Guru;
> it's the blessing of power and strength of life!

(11)
Let it please the women, our beloved daughters,
> whose hearts and minds are filled with a great affection.

let's make good beer.
[Refrain]
It's the blessing of the Guru;
> it's the blessing of power and strength of life.

As it was in the beginning, let's make good beer
It's the blessing of the Guru;
        it's the blessing of power and strength of life!
(12)
As it was in the beginning, let's make good beer.
When you gesture respectfully in invitation,
that you might offer both food and drink,
let's make good beer.
[Repeat Refrain]
(13)
As it was in the beginning, let's make good beer.
When the affection of the women, our beloved daughters, is great,
with their own hands they respectfully offer both food and drink.
When inviting with the karsyol beer-offering
        marked with pure unclarified butter,
do make the beer well.
[Repeat Refrain]
(14)
As it was in the beginning, let's make good beer.
When inviting the wife's elder brother (?) Syorap
        who lives in the east to come,
do make the beer well.
[Repeat Refrain]
(15)
As it was in the beginning, let's make good beer.
When inviting the red Dabgyal from the south to come,
do make the beer well.
[Repeat Refrain]
(16)
As it was in the beginning, let's make good beer.
When inviting elder brother Nawa Thaya from the west,
        elder brother Dorje Lhekpa, King of Hrosyang Ma, to come,
do make the beer well.
[Repeat Refrain]
(17)
As it was in the beginning, let's make good beer.
When inviting the old Nharu Pencho from the north,
        wife's elder brother (?) Kukang, to come,
do make the beer well.
[Repeat Refrain]

(18)

When the hearts and minds of the women, our beloved daughters,
    are filled with a great affection,
do make the beer well.
[Repeat Refrain]
(19)

When the affection in your heart and mind is great,
when you gesture respectfully in invitation,
do make the beer well.
[Repeat Refrain]
(20)

As it was in the beginning, let's make good beer
When you gesture respectfully in invitation,
when you invite with snacks and drink,
do make the beer well.
[Repeat Refrain]
(21)

As it was in the beginning, let's make good beer;
do make the beer well.
When inviting with a pure karsyol with butter on it,
do make the beer well.
[Repeat Refrain]
(22)

As it was in the beginning, let's make good beer;
do make the beer well.
When inviting the earth divinity to come,
do make the beer well.
[Repeat Refrain]
(23)

As it was in the beginning, let's make good beer;
do make the beer well.
When inviting the divinities and divine serpent [la-klu], Neta Shipta,
    the earth divinity of the village to come,
do make the beer well.
[Repeat Refrain]
(24)

As it was in the beginning, let's make good beer;
do make the beer well.
When inviting the Kali Goddess of the Waters
    and the Great God of the Meadows to come,
do make the beer well.

[Repeat Refrain]
(25)
As it was in the beginning, let's make good beer.
When inviting the Serpent Goddess, the Water Goddess,
    and the Brahmacharya Sitta Mahadeo, to come,
do make the beer well.
[Repeat Refrain]
(26)
As it was in the beginning, let's make good beer;
do make the beer well.
When inviting the god husband (?) Mhiktung,
    or the god wife's elder brother (?) Konchyo to come,
do make the beer well.
[Repeat Refrain]
(27)
As it was in the beginning, let's make good beer;
do make the beer well.
When inviting the Digin Lama to come,
do make the beer well.
[Repeat Refrain]
(28)
As it was in the beginning, let's make good beer;
do make the beer well.
Let the mouth be not empty,
let the hand be not empty,
by hand have I placed these precious offerings
    (for casting a horoscope).
do make the beer well.
[Repeat Refrain]
(29)
As it was in the beginning, let's make good beer;
do make the beer well.
When inviting the woman saint Khaisyur of Gobbo Hill to come,
do make the beer well.
[Repeat Refrain]
(30)
When the affection in your heart and mind is great,
do make the beer well.
[Repeat Refrain]
(31)
As it was in the beginning, let's make good beer;

do make the beer well.
When inviting with a pure karsyol with butter on it,
do make the beer well.
[Repeat Refrain]
(32)
As it was in the beginning, let's make good beer;
do make the beer well.
When inviting the Newar woman TuDi to come,
when requesting fulsome harvests to come to you,
do make the beer well.
[Repeat Refrain]
(33)
As it was in the beginning, let's make good beer;
do make the beer well.
When inviting the divinity of (?) Ganesh Lake to come,
do make the beer well.
[Repeat Refrain]
(34)
As it was in the beginning, let's make good beer;
do make the beer well.
When inviting the earth divinity of the village to come,
do make the beer well.
[Repeat Refrain]
(35)
As it was in the beginning, let's make good beer;
do make the beer well.
When inviting the Great God Saraswati of Jaisur,
    the great self-born divinity, to come,
do make the beer well.
[Repeat Refrain]
(36)
As it was in the beginning, let's make good beer.
Let the mouth be not empty,
let the hand be not empty,
by hand have I placed these precious offerings
    (for casting a horoscope).
Let's make good beer.
[Repeat Refrain]
(37)
As it was in the beginning, let's make good beer;
do make the beer well.

When inviting Lama Konchyo, Life Konchyo,
    Hyonden Konchyo, Ngying Tsen, Barimo Konchyo,
    when requesting fulsome harvests to come to you,
do make the beer well.
[Repeat Refrain]
(38)
When the affection in your heart and mind is great,
when you gesture respectfully in invitation,
do make the beer well.
It's the blessing of the Guru;
    it's the blessing of power and strength of life.
As it was in the beginning, let's make good beer.
It's the blessing of the Guru;
    it's the blessing of power and strength of life.

REFERENCES

Baal, Jan van (1975). "The Part of Women in the Marriage Trade: Objects or Behaving as Objects." In Baal, ed., *Reciprocity and the Position of Women*, pp. 70–96.

Fürer-Haimendorf, Christoph von (1964). *The Sherpas of Nepal: Buddhist Highlanders*. London: Murray.

Holmberg, David H. (1980). "Lama, Shaman, and Lambu in Tamang Religious Practice." Ph.D. diss., Cornell University.

March, Kathryn S. (1979). "The Intermediacy of Women: Female Gender Symbolism and the Social Position of Women among Tamangs and Sherpas of Highland Nepal." Ph.D. diss., Cornell University.

March, Kathryn S. (1984). "Weaving, Writing, and Gender." *Man* 18: 729–44.

Mauss, Marcel (1967). *The Gift*. Trans. I. Cunnison. New York: Norton.

Ortner, Sherry B. (1972). "A Kernel of Truth: Some Notes on the Analysis of Connotation." *Semiotica* 6(4): 324–43.

Ortner, Sherry B. (1978). *Sherpas through Their Rituals*. Cambridge: Cambridge University Press.

Sahlins, Marshall (1979). *Stone Age Economics*. New York: Aldine.

FEEDING THEIR FAITH: RECIPE KNOWLEDGE AMONG THAI BUDDHIST WOMEN

Penny Van Esterik

Southeast Asia, while noted for its tasty cuisine, has no comparable reputation for tantalizing analyses of food symbolism. Unlike South Asia, where Hindu ideology has stimulated sophisticated studies of Indian food symbolism (e.g., Marriott 1964; Babb 1970), Buddhist Southeast Asia has no significant literature on food meanings. This lack of elaboration reflects the limited concern with food in Buddhist ideology; however, interesting questions about women, food, and Buddhism can be raised when we examine familiar questions from an unfamiliar perspective—the culinary perspective. In this article I examine how Thai Buddhist women use their knowledge of food to define categories of natural and supernatural beings, mark changes in ritual time, and address significant intellectual and practical problems posed by the doctrine of Theravada Buddhism.

THE SETTING[1]

Crocodile Village straddles the highway linking important marketing towns in Suphanburi province, west central Thailand. Composed of scattered hamlets surrounded by rice fields, the overgrown village is larger and wealthier than many in the district. With its own market center, school, and newly built Buddhist temple, it has inhabitants justifiably proud of their material and spiritual resources. The villagers grow rice and other crops, raise cattle, sell household necessities, and offer their labor for daily wages whenever possible. Traditional Thai-style teak houses raised off the ground alternate with garish Bangkok-style, pastel frame houses squeezed into any available space between the older compounds. A network of narrow paths winds around the compounds, with the principal roads leading to the market and the temple. On all but the busiest days of transplanting or harvesting rice, groups of neighbors may be seen in the small coffee shops and noodle stalls in the market. In the kitchens behind the houses women prepare rice and side dishes to meet the nutritional, social, and ritual needs of their households.

The resources and planning required to prepare food for human and non-human consumption take up a great deal of village women's time and energy. Occasionally food is prepared and offered communally, by many women acting together. If food is prepared for the monastery, women enjoy the leftovers together. As householders they prepare food for monks during their early morning rounds, and as individuals they request help from a variety of spiritual sources. In these and other food-mediated actions women employ their extensive knowledge of Theravada Buddhism.

BUDDHIST KNOWLEDGE

The dominant religious tradition of present-day Sri Lanka, Burma, Thailand, Laos, and Kampuchea, Theravada Buddhism is a community-based religion practiced in rural areas as well as elite urban royal centers such as Bangkok. Its rituals use Pali texts and are performed both by members of the monastic order (collectively, the *sangha*) and by devout laypersons. Both lay and monastic Buddhism are guided by the law of Karma: all actions are conditioned by antecedent causes. For laypersons, making merit is the most important religious act. Merit is made by giving (*dāna*), keeping Buddhist moral precepts (*sīla*), and mental development (*bhāvanā*).[2]

Analysts who distinguish between folk or popular Buddhism and canonical or scriptural Buddhism—between the Great Tradition and the Little Tradition—characterize rural Theravadins as animists possessing an incomplete or simplified understanding of Buddhism. While this approach has been criticized (cf. Tambiah 1970; Lehman 1972), its underlying assumption of qualitative and quantitative differences in the distribution of Buddhist knowledge both within and among communities is useful. Spiro (1966) accounts for variation by determining differences in the levels at which knowledge is internalized. Although many principles influence the distribution of this knowledge in Thailand, both men and women assume that men have more opportunities than women do to obtain canonical knowledge. Thai women regularly prefaced their discussions about Buddhism with the suggestion that if I really wanted to understand Buddhism, I should talk to men—preferably men who had been monks.

Male specialists—monks—know more, or are assumed to know more, than laywomen. Laymen who have once been monks should know more than men who have never been ordained. Most Thai men acquire knowledge of Buddhism through participation in rituals requiring recitation of Pali texts; fewer women have this opportunity, and consequently fewer women can recite from these texts. Notable exceptions to this generalization are the *maē chī* or "women in white," erroneously referred to as Buddhist nuns. The term *chī* is probably related to the Sanskrit root *jiv*, to be alive (Terweil 1975, p. 258). These specialized laywomen wear white, keep eight precepts, and live together in a community often near a temple.

On the other hand, women generally outnumber men in attendance at weekly temple services and in the observance of the eight precepts, particularly during the rains retreat (Pali, *vassa*), as many ethnographers have noted (e.g., Kirsch 1975, p. 184; Tambiah 1976, p. 308; Terweil 1975, p. 210). Throughout the history of Buddhism generous laywomen have supplied the monastic order with sons, land and the necessities of life. An inscription from the turn of the fifteenth century in the Thai Buddhist state of Sukhodaya records a widow's generosity to a particular monk: "Because of our zeal we prepared food in great abundance (to place) in front of his lordship and all the monks, and we lifted up the food to present to them in this areca grove" (Griswold and Na Nagara 1979, pp. 71–72).

In Thailand, and probably elsewhere, men and women experience Buddhism differently: men from the sharply defined contrasts of monastic life, constrained by rules explicating every aspect of daily life, and transmitted through the memorization of Pali texts; and women from the more personal, less sharply bounded perspective of ritual participant and merit maker. For women, Buddhist belief and practice is more a part of everyday life, more directly enmeshed in the world of experience.

FOOD AS SYMBOL

Context-specific religious knowledge converges with everyday knowledge in the domain of food. What properties of food substances make them suitable antecedent objects for symbolic elaboration? Foods come in discrete, named units that are divisible and can be shared. They are describable by reference to several sensory attributes—smell, color, taste. They are common products, used everyday, but critically necessary since our lives depend on food. Foods are valued, and we usually have an emotional response to them, both idiosyncratic responses based on personal experiences and culturally defined responses—repugnance for eating insects, for example. Foods are usually combined and ordered into recipes for dishes, courses, meals, and sequences of meals. Food can be changed in form by human intervention (raw, cooked, rotted, fried, boiled). These different processing techniques change the characteristics of food substances in easily identifiable ways. Food substances can be varied in both quantity and quality, which makes them suitable for marking differences in status or prestige of both people and events. The consumption of food leaves an easily visible mark on a human. Both starvation and over-indulgence in food are easily communicated to the public. These attributes of food make them suitable antecedent objects for symbolic elaboration. In Sperber's terminology, this is the substantial base that derives from the natural and material properties of food used as symbol (Sperber 1975, p. 13).

Anthropologists building on structuralist arguments demonstrate that foods convey symbolic messages. Both meals and categories of food have a definable structure, and the patterns so formed carry substantial social and cultural meanings (e.g., Douglas 1972, 1981; Firth 1973). But the links between the domains of food and religion remain poorly defined because relations between the domains are mediated by women. Knowledge of food in most societies, including Thailand, is in the heads and hands of women and is transmitted through women, for women possess everyday knowledge of food processing and preparation. This recipe knowledge is pragmatic competence in routine performance (Berger and Luckmann 1967, p. 45).

Women as transmitters of food knowledge participate actively in interpreting and manipulating Buddhist paradoxes, although their mode of religious expression has been less frequently captured ethnographically. Indeed, women's religious lives have only recently begun to be explored systematically. In writing of the everyday concerns of women in different religious traditions, Falk and Gross find "there is no tension between their religious and their mundane lives. Rather, their religious concerns validate these women's ordinary concerns and help to give them meaning" (1980, p. 71). Thai women's use of food demonstrates the complexity and depth of their religious knowledge and devotion.

FOOD TRANSACTIONS

In rural Thai society people control others by feeding them. Food transactions define social relationships among humans and between humans and other classes of beings. Women process, prepare, and usually present these food offerings, and the knowledge of appropriate foods and recipes is passed on orally from mothers to daughters.

The relationship established by feeding others is a voluntary one. If you have never given food to persons in need, or to a guardian spirit, for example, then you have never set up a relationship with them and thus have no responsibility toward them. You can safely ignore that person or spirit. But once you begin feeding a person or spirit, you must continue to provide food. If you stop, you are in trouble, for it is dangerous to break off a relationship once it has been established. Better never to have offered food in the first place than to stop feeding!

Women distribute food to many categories of human and superhuman entities. A woman who is a "good nourisher" is admired in rural Thai society. An ideal Thai woman supports both individuals and institutions with food, as the following examples will illustrate.

Humans

In Crocodile Village the nutritional and social needs of infants are met by breast-feeding, an act of loving kindness that establishes a reciprocal relation between mothers and children. Ideally, a son repays this obligation by ordaining as a monk and the youngest daughter by remaining in the parental household to care for her parents in their old age. The ritual texts spoken at the preordination ceremony for monks, and at tonsure ceremonies where children have their topknots ritually cut, begin by emphasizing the degree of obligation children have to their mothers who provided them with milk. As this first natural food, human milk, is replaced by a cultural food, rice, the child joins the rest of the family in consuming meals prepared by women. By consuming rice, a child gradually becomes Thai. Relatives and occasional visitors are welcome to share family meals and hospitality.

Women regularly prepare food for religious and community ritual. This communal activity allows several women to share the merit accumulated by food preparation and binds participating women into a single moral community. This community is most clearly seen as women pass food dishes back and forth before the dishes are presented to monks. Since women cannot hand anything directly to monks, men generally arrange the food dishes prepared by women and hand the utensils to the monks.

Food transactions also serve as temporal boundary markers, marking the passage of an individual through the life cycle and the passage of time through a yearly cycle. The rituals marking an individual's passage through life are not, with the exception of funerals, the concern of Buddhist monks. These ritual occasions may provide an opportunity for merit making, but the rituals themselves are Brahmanic in origin and derived from Vedic personal rites of passage, as the food offerings emphasize. For example, rice mixed with sweetened condensed milk, or with coconut milk and sugar, is the basis of boiled red and white desserts important for rites of passage such as birthdays, tonsures, marriages, and preordination rites. These brightly colored desserts, auspicious and pure foods, are offered to guardian spirits as well as to the Brahman practitioner and the monks who come to preach following household celebrations. These ritual rites of passage require an individual's *khwan* (soul) to be anchored firmly in his or her body. To complete this ritual task, women prepare a conical "tree" with offerings of cooked rice, bananas, boiled eggs, and desserts. Like the deities, human souls prefer vegetarian food.

Deceased Humans

Women also prepare food for deceased ancestors in order to control the "connectedness" of the living and dead. On occasions of household rituals, ancestors are given small trays to sample all the food dishes prepared— bananas, coconut, boiled rice, meat dishes, sweets, and occasionally whiskey. By feeding the ancestors these particular foods, women are treating them as deceased humans who reside in one of the Buddhist hells or as free-floating spirits between rebirth states. These ghosts or *phī* are placated by food offerings (*līang phī*), not worshiped. They are treated as potentially disruptive guests at family celebrations.

Women also prepare additional food for the monks and share the accumulated merit with the deceased through a ritual called *kraut nam*, which extends merit to deceased ancestors by ritually pouring water from one vessel to another or onto the ground. Villagers often reported dreaming of deceased relatives who were hungry in one of the Buddhist hells. The deceased relatives requested their descendants to feed the monks and share the merit with them. Women who do not provide food for the monks in this life will reap the consequences and starve in their next life.

Funerals are marked by the use of puffed rice, which is strewn on a path following a funeral procession, since "death is like puffed rice which can't be planted to grow again" (Tambiah 1970, p. 156).

The most elaborate cooked food is prepared for the half-year festival of *Sāat Thai* (Pali, *sarada*, autumn). Held in September, this three-day celebration reunites village members who reside outside the village. During this time the souls of deceased ancestors return to earth and are honored communally. Men and boys who seldom attend temple services present substantial amounts of cooked food prepared by their wives and mothers to the monks, in addition to raw rice and fruit. (For a discussion of the equivalent royal ritual, see Quaritch Wales 1931).

The celebration resembles a first-fruits ritual where the best of the harvest is offered to the temple. Women prepare two special dishes for the occasion. The first, *krayasat*, is a mixture of cooked new rice, peanuts, sesame seeds, dried rice, puffed rice, and coconut, held together by palm sugar or sweetened condensed milk. Krayasat prepared for Sāt Thai resembles dry, sweet offerings common in South India, the *panchakadjaya* (five foods) or *ettangadi* (eight foods). The confection consists of jaggery, coconut, puffed rice, sesame, and several other variable ingredients (Ferro-Luzzi 1977, p. 513). Historical continuity with Indian food patterns can be seen in some of these narrowly defined ritual contexts within Buddhist communities. Groups of women prepare the mixture under their houses in huge pans. Identical plates of the confection are then exchanged among households. Clients present plates to their patrons, and young people rush to present the sweets to their elder relatives and to the monks.

The second dish is *kanom chin*, a fine rice noodle prepared with a sour spicy fish sauce. The fish mixture is the favorite food of ghosts and spirits and is offered to guardian spirits when they are treated as *phī*. The fine noodles are particularly enjoyed by *phī pret*, a category of ghosts with only a tiny hole for a mouth—large enough to consume fine noodles.

Monks

Monks and laity follow two different routes to salvation, but these paths are linked by food exchanges. Ideally, food offerings to monks are characterized by formality, distance, and impersonality. Women generally offer cooked rice as the monks make their early morning rounds. On holy days women place cooked rice in the bowls of all community monks and offer the best supplementary food dish they can afford to prepare—a meat or fish curry, stir-fried vegetables, or sweet desserts, for example. Food must be served in the best bowl owned by the family and kept for this purpose, and no one may taste or sniff the dishes before they are presented to the monks. If laypersons smelled or tasted the dishes before presenting them to the monks, they might lose their intention to give freely and completely, experiencing a degree of reluctance in giving up delicious food.

Food served to the monks is identical to food served to the unordained except that the best and most expensive supplementary dishes are prepared. Women are well aware of the additional merit accruing from feeding monks, a sentiment also expressed in Burma: "The feeding of a hundred laymen is equivalent to the feeding of one novice; the feeding of one hundred novices is equivalent to that of one ordinary monk" (Spiro 1970, p. 109).

Food offerings for monks also serve us useful temporal markers, distinguishing the four holy days in a lunar month from ordinary "weekdays." Monks are restricted to receiving cooked food in the mornings. Foods offered to the monks after the noonday fast are presented in their raw form. Similarly, when large stores of food are given during the annual cycle of Buddhist holidays, raw foods are presented. Raw rice and uncooked fruits are given to monks at the beginning (July) and end (October) of the rain's retreat (Pali, *vassa*) and at the New Year celebration. Presenting food in its raw, unprocessed form does not challenge monastic discipline, which specifies that a monk may not keep or store cooked food after the noonday fast. Uncooked food is most often presented by males.

Buddha Image

Crocodile villagers treated the Buddha image in the preaching hall not as another monk but as a deity (*thēwadā*) and provided it with a tray for rice and a sample of vegetable dishes, fruit, and desserts. The best and most attractive dishes were reserved for the Buddha. One woman from the community carried the tray and placed it near the image before the monks began their morning chants on the Buddhist holy days. This food was not eaten by the laity after the service but rather was thrown to the pigs, since humans should not partake of food offered to the deities.

The Buddha image is a focal point for the ritual cycle of Buddhist holidays throughout the year. Key events in the Buddha's biography are reenacted ritually—his birth, enlightenment, and death, as if Buddhist communities experience a constant present time.

Deities

Food offerings prepared for the Brahman gods in Bangkok, and for the deities invited to the village for ritual occasions, are always vegetarian, reflecting quite explicitly their Hindu origin. These gods may be invited by name—Indra, Brahma—or as a general category of Hindu gods converted to Buddhism who offer benevolent protection to those practicing Buddhist morality. Vegetarian offerings include bananas, coconut, cooked rice, puffed rice, green peas, sesame seeds, and red and white boiled sweets. These vegetarian food offerings to the Buddha and the deities are referred to as *kryang bucha* and are a form of ritual worship.

Many supernatural beings fall into the ambiguous category of guardian spirits. Guardian spirits can be interpreted as deities (*thē wadā*) or ghosts (*phī*), as I have argued elsewhere (P. Van Esterik 1982), and are treated accordingly. On the many occasions when guardian spirits are invoked for protection of temple, house, or city, appropriate food offerings are prepared for them. Once again the pragmatic knowledge necessary for this very routine performance resides with women, who prepare the appropriate combinations of foods.

The guardian spirit of the temple compound is believed to be the spirit of a former abbot of the temple. His image sits a few inches lower than the Buddha image in the preaching hall. He is a vegetarian, and a number of villagers felt that the Buddha tray, placed casually between the two images, was really meant for the former abbot and not the Buddha. The guardian spirit of the village, on the other hand, ate meat curries, chewed betel, smoked tobacco, and drank whiskey. *Nang māj*, the guardian spirit residing in wood, and more particularly in the house post, is given bananas, coconut, and desserts—but no meat or fish.

The guardian of individual house compounds is given foods appropriate for a ghost. When necessary, village women prepare a special dish of fish, fish oils, peppers, and lime, which ghosts particularly enjoy. To illustrate the complexity of food offerings to guardian spirits, consider the foods prepared for the installation of a guardian spirit of a house. This spirit is labeled *phī chao thī, chao thī, phī ban Phra Phum, Phra Phum chao thī*, or *Phra Chai Mong Khon*, depending on how much knowledge the villager has of the spirit domain and whether the spirit is considered a deity or a ghost (cf. P. Van Esterik 1982).

On this ritual occasion, a guardian spirit house was being installed in the northeast corner of a new compound. In a small, open, "eye-level" altar decorated with red and white flags and flowers, the spirit was offered incense, a conical offering made of folded banana leaves, water, and miniature plates of food offerings. The four plates held betel nut, sour and spicy fish with rice, desserts, and water, arranged clockwise from the image of the guardian spirit located at the back of the house (see Figure 1).

In front of the spirit house a ritual practitioner arranged additional offerings for the guardian spirit. A pig's head was flanked by a whole fish on the left and a whole chicken on the right. Dishes of meat curry and red and white boiled desserts sat in front of the pig's head. Both the curries and the boiled desserts require substantial preparation on the part of household women, but the food intended for spirits is not eaten by humans. The stability of this particular configuration of offerings is of considerable historical interest, since the arrangement of fish, pig, and chicken offered to a

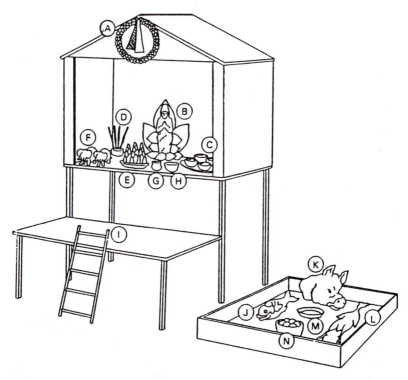

Figure 1 Offerings for the Guardian Spirit of the House Compound. (A) Red and white flags and flower wreath; (B) statue of guardian spirit; (C) tray containing dishes of betel nut, rice and fish, dessert and water; (D) incense; (E) baisi (offering of folded banana leaves); (F) elephant dolls; (G) oil; (H) water; (I) ladder for spirit; (J) fish; (K) pig's head; (L) chicken; (M) curry; (N) desserts.

guardian spirit communicates to a Southeast Asian audience broader than just the ritual specialists of rural Thailand. Loeffler (1968) has proposed that the arrangement represents earth between sky and water, represented by the most prominent food sources in each region. He illustrates a scene of an old death ritual in Shantung, China, showing a pig's head flanked by a fish on the left side and a fowl on the right. Using configurations from various parts of Southeast Asia, he connects the fish symbol to the prenatal state and the bird symbol to the postmortal state. These symbols may retain their structure in a Buddhist context where, for example, the *naga*, an embodiment of water and the underworld, becomes a protector of Buddhism.

WRESTLING WITH PARADOX

Food defines categories of spirits and provides strategies for dealing with these categories through ritual worship or placation using food offerings. Food also sets temporal boundaries marking changes in an individual's status and reenacting the events of the Buddha's life throughout the year. In these ethnographic examples food is used to distinguish between different kinds of natural and supernatural entities. The contrast between vegetarian and nonvegetarian offerings differentiates gods that have a place in the Hindu pantheon from humans and ghosts. The vegetarian offerings for the gods feature fruit and sweet desserts often made with coconut milk or sweetened condensed milk, paralleling the Hindu distinction between pure deities who accept only vegetarian offerings and impure (often local) deities who prefer cooked meat, alcohol, and narcotics.

But the Buddhist world order is filled with hierarchically arranged categories of beings, from the depths of the various hells to the realms of various gods. For mortals, the identification and interpretation of other beings is problematic. Consider the problem of feeding deceased ancestors or guardian spirits. They may be treated and fed as deities or as ghosts, depending on the interpretation of the householder; the categories are ambiguous. Possible ambiguity also surrounds the offerings to the Buddha statue. Should the Buddha be treated as a deity and given vegetarian offerings? In Crocodile Village the plate of food offered to the Buddha contained only rice, vegetables, and fruit, suggesting that the Buddha is interpreted as a deity. Yet in northeast Thailand both monks and Buddha images are given meat curries (Tambiah 1970, p. 341), suggesting that the Buddha is interpreted more as a monk-teacher.

Concern for the appropriate food offerings for spirits parallels the domestic dilemma surrounding the consumption of meat. Meat dishes require killing, an act that clearly violates Buddhist precepts. But meat dishes are presented to monks, and meat is not explicitly forbidden to them according to the Vinaya rules of the monastic order. In the *Majjhima Nīkaya* the Buddha expressly forbids animal meat only if it is seen, heard, or suspected to have been killed on purpose to make a dish for a monk (Horner 1970, p. 33). Indeed, the texts even specify that the Buddha "eat the proper proportion of curry to rice, experiencing flavor but not greed for flavor" (Horner 1970, p. 324). (Recall, too, that the Buddha died after eating a meal of pork.)

Meat eating is interpreted by the Buddhist laity in more than one way. Thai villagers argue that monks should not be given meat dishes since they require killing, which breaks Buddhist precepts. This is the interpretation made by the Sinhalese who give only vegetarian food offerings to the

Buddha, monks, and gods (Yalman 1969, p. 88). Monks, then, may refuse to accept gifts if they know that precepts have been broken by the donor. By turning the begging bowl upside down they are exercising their right and even obligation to censure evil conduct on the part of the laity (Spiro 1970, p. 410). Yet I never saw monks refuse food from a layperson. Vegetarian offerings may be seen as purer and more appropriate for monks, since deities as precept keepers also receive vegetarian offerings; the poor who cannot afford to present meat dishes favor this interpretation.

On the other hand, meat dishes may be consumed by monks simply because they are required to accept any food offering presented to them without making distinctions or showing preferences. In this interpretation the responsibility of the monk to accept the laity's offerings overrides his role as precept keeper. Since meat is the most expensive food item available to Thai villagers, a gift of a meat curry, for example, involves the greatest sacrifice, and *dāna* (charity) requires giving freely without holding back.

Within Buddhist argumentation, then, meat eating could be explained as both appropriate and not appropriate for a monk. Women rehearse this problem daily as they prepare food for the monks, constantly observing what dishes others are bringing to the temple. On Buddhist holidays news of what dishes we had prepared for the monks always preceded us to the temple. Toward the end of our fieldwork, as our funds diminished, I recall trying to argue for the purity and appropriateness of our vegetarian offerings to a very skeptical and wealthy neighbor.

The contradiction between feminine generous giving of food to the monks and masculine ascetic rejection of such sensuous pleasures as eating lies at the heart of Buddhist belief and practice. It demands constant interpretation and reinterpretation by generations of Buddhist believers. Analysts cannot afford to overlook any domain where these interpretations are made.

The problem constantly raised concerns the public nature of selfless and generous feeding and can be traced to the texts of canonical Buddhism. Without doubt, generous public giving is meritorious. In the *Sangutta Nikaya* we read:

> This food both gods and men chiefly desire
> Whom may that creature be, demon or spirit,
> Who, unlike them, hankers not after food?

> The food that's given in faith with heart made pure
> That finds him out in this world and the next.
>   (Rhys-Davids 1971, p. 43)

The sentiment is clear: householders who give food offerings will be rewarded in their future lives, those who do not will suffer. The same sentiment was expressed less elegantly in a Thai woman's dream. She dreamed that at the end of a market day she had one rotten banana left over and gave it to a monk. She dreamed she died, went to hell, and had only rotten bananas to eat, although she could see others eating good food. Waking from her dream, she immediately prepared the best food dishes she could afford to give to the monks.

The story of Sujata presenting rice milk to the Buddha before his enlightenment illustrates the care and devotion women expend on food offerings. The milk Sujata used was obtained by feeding the milk of 500 cows to 250 cows, and so on down to feeding the milk of 16 cows to 8. "The working the milk in and in ... was done to increase the thickness and sweetness and the strength-giving properties of the milk" (Warren 1969, p. 72). As Sujata's food offering illustrates, charity should be selfless and performed with right intention. Such an act should logically be unpublicized, unrecognized, and not done for personal aggrandizement. But in Thai communities meritorious giving is always done publicly and loudly, with the amount or quality of the gift announced over a loudspeaker or recorded with a flourish in temple records. Neighbors know who prepared or organized food offerings for the monks or who cleaned up after a meal. Clearly, merit-making acts in Thai communities are public social statements as well as private religious ones. The public nature of merit making is proof that a gift is given freely: "It is considered more likely that one has had good intentions if the merit making is public. In fact, if the act of giving is not public it may not be considered an act of merit but rather a personal relationship, a 'deal' between the giver and receiver which may be suspect" (J. Van Esterik 1977, p. 98). Since the amount of merit accumulated from an act of *dāna* depends on the spiritual worth of the giver, the giver's worth must be made apparent and validated publicly.

While laywomen express their devotion by preparing and presenting food to the monks, the monks are admonished to take food "with reflection and judgement, not for sport, not for indulgence, not for personal charm, not for beautifying but just enough for the support, for the upkeep of the body" (Woodward 1973, p. 149). This emphasis on moderation and control in eating developed from the Buddha's rejection of the ascetic path of semistarvation.

The rules of the monastic order include specifications about how monks should eat. These rules serve to define the monastic community positively as those who reside together and eat communally. Excommunication, moreover, means that a monk can no longer partake of the communal meal. The distinction between *āmisasambhoga* (communion in eating) and *dharmasambhogakāya* (communion in the law) is based in part on rules of eating. The meaning of *āmisasambhoga* might also be extended to refer to the communal merit making and commensality of the laity (cf. Mus 1978, pp. 263–64, 289–90).

A Thai commentary on the rules explains this concern:

> Wrong mental states easily come to the surface during the collecting or eating of food unless both mind and body are well-guarded. These rules are all concerned with various kinds of bodily restraint to be observed. The sight of *bhikkus* eating their food is one activity of theirs which householders have a chance to observe...(Nanomali 1966, p. 116).

Women are particularly observant of monks when they eat. But the response of monks to their food is also problematic for women. For if monks show obvious enjoyment of the food presented, the donor knows that the monk has accepted the gift and that merit has been made. But a monk who shows enjoyment of food is less worthy of the gift. If a monk does not show enjoyment of the food or happens to pass over that dish, women are unsure whether their gift has been rejected or whether the monk is exhibiting ideal self-control. A monk who shows minimal interest in food is the more worthy, but by his self-control he provides the donor with no evidence of having accepted the gift. Perhaps this uncertainty is why women give food dishes to a number of different monks in an attempt to balance worthiness of recipient with evidence of the acceptance of the food.

This paradox exists because food is also used as a metaphor for the foulness of the body. "All beings are persisters by food" (Woodward 1972, p. 35). Monks are admonished to concentrate on the repulsiveness of food and become conscious of "the cloying of food" (Hare 1973, p. 68). "From the arising of food is the arising of body; from the ceasing of food is the ceasing of body" (Woodward 1954, p. 51).

The Burmese also recognize the paradox arising from the constant generous giving of food to the monks: "the greater his rejection of worldly goods, the holier the monk is deemed to be, but the holier he is, the more lavishly he is supplied with worldly goods" (Spiro 1970, p. 414).

CONCLUSION

At the first light of dawn the sounds in Crocodile Village confirm that another culinary cycle has begun. Charcoal fires support a pot of the best rice the household has available; women and young girls pound peppers and shred coconut for curries. By the time the line of Buddhist monks passes silently in front of the house, the rest of the family is ready to share in the merit accrued from feeding the monks by touching the bowl or the spoon the woman uses to make her offering. The food she prepares is the means for increasing her own spiritual worth and that of her family; but it nourishes more than her faith, as the leftovers provide the best meal her family may consume that day.

Cooking and eating are activities that cut across the artificial oppositions of domestic and monastic, this world and other world, and Great Tradition and Little Tradition so common in studies of Theravada Buddhism. Using women's perceptions about religious action allows us to obtain a more complete view of the religious field than is possible by focusing only on men's more visible religious roles.

Thai Buddhist women must know a great deal about Theravada Buddhism in order to make culturally appropriate food offerings. More significantly, the correct use of food offerings and exchanges requires constant interpretation and reinterpretation of principles and meanings, some of which are based on significant intellectual problems within Theravada Buddhism. Food is not the only domain where these problems are dealt with. On the contrary, these problems arise in other domains, and other Buddhists grapple with them (cf. Ortner 1975, for the Sherpa; Aung Thwin 1979, for the Burmese). But food is an ideal medium for expressing the ambiguity the contradiction implicit in the practice of religion. As an antecedent object, food is easily available, is infinitely varied in its transformations, and accumulates layers of associated meanings, providing enough historical specificity to tempt speculations about broad cultural processes. How did food and eating lose its caste restrictions in Southeast Asia while Brahmanic ritual was retained? Why are offerings to guardian spirits necessary in a world ordered by the laws of Karma? If feeding someone gives you power over them, how do women use this power in their interactions with men?

Food is the basis for interaction with the whole range of sentient beings who populate the Buddhist cosmos—the layers of hells, the realms of animals, guardian spirits, other humans, and deities, and the dimly perceived nothingness of nirvana. The links between givers and receivers of food are symbolic, and the manipulation of these symbols is in the hands and heads of women. Food offerings create and recreate the categories for conceptualizing the order of the cosmos. By doing so, they also mark the passage of time, for the quality of time in Buddhist order is cyclical; the agricultural cycle provides both the raw materials and the timing for seasonal rituals.

Even life-cycle rituals stretch out through many lifetimes, as the cycle of rebirths generates countless opportunities for growth and decay. By defining categories of beings, and cycles of time, food interactions reinforce the total cosmology of Thai Buddhism and place women as key social actors at the center of Buddhist action.

NOTES

1. In 1971 my husband and I spent 8 months in Crocodile Village, preparing a general ethnographic description of a post-peasant community. We began studying related problems regarding the growth of lay Buddhist meditation movements and the relation between Buddhist and Brahmanic ritual in the village. These projects required attendance at all community rituals and detailed interviews with the village "experts" on religion. Our informants included monks, ex-monks, ritual specialists, laypersons who helped organize and carry out rituals, and people attending the rituals. We planned for interviews by preparing broad, open-ended questions or problems to discuss with acknowledged authorities. These interviews elicited normative rules and post hoc explanations for ritual acts. This background, combined with attendance at ritual events and subsequent discussions evaluating the performance, provided more balance between ideal models and actual behavior.

   During preparation for ritual events, and even well into the early stages of rituals, I sat with village women helping them prepare food, and being roundly scolded for suggesting inappropriate combinations or arrangements, while my husband sat with men and monks discussing Buddhist doctrine. It was not until my return from the field and my subsequent reading and research in nutritional anthropology that I realized how much of my understanding of Brahmanic and Buddhist ritual, guardian spirits, and village social interaction generally came through these food-mediated experiences buried in my daily journals. In spite of additional fieldwork on infant feeding in that community in the following year, and my husband's more intensive dissertation research on meditation movements (J. Van Esterik 1977), I did not conduct more intensive, focused research of food in that community. Instead, I have turned to secondary sources, Buddhist texts, and our photographs to construct the argument developed here.

2. It is not necessary to know a great deal about Theravada Buddhism in order to follow the argument of this paper. Good overviews of Theravada Buddhism as it is practiced in Thailand are presented in Tambiah (1970) and Terweil (1975).

   Buddhism, both Theravada and Mahayana, is based on the life of Gotama who was born in north India in 563 B.C. Among the several different schools existing in the first centuries B.C., the most lasting division is between the Mahayana tradition, which spread north through Tibet, China, and East Asia, and the Theravada tradition of Southeast Asia. The Theravada texts, written in Pali in the first century A.D., and later commentaries on them remain the basis for present-day services and education for monks. The faithful take refuge in the Buddha, the compassionate teacher, the Dhamma, his teachings, and the Sangha, the monastic order he founded.

   Theravada Buddhism is a community-oriented religion emphasizing moral conduct, support of the monastic order, and good works rather than the more esoteric, ascetic routes to personal salvation associated with Mahayana Buddhism.

REFERENCES

Aung Thwin, Michael (1979). "The Role of Sasana Reform in Burmese History: Economic Dimensions of Religion Purification." *Journal of Asian Studies*, 28: 671–88.

Babb, L. A. (1970). "The Food for the Gods in Chhattisgarh: Some Structural Features of Hindu Ritual." *Southwestern Journal of Anthropology*, 26: 287–304.

Berger, P. L., and T. Luckmann (1967). *The Social Construction of Reality*. Garden City, N.Y.: Doubleday.

Douglas, Mary (1972). "Deciphering a Meal." *Daedalus*, no. 101: 61–81.

——— (1981). "Food and Culture: Measuring the Intricacy of Rule Systems." *Social Science Information*, 20: 1–35.

Falk, Nancy, and Rita Gross (1980). *Unspoken Worlds*. San Francisco: Harper & Row.

Ferro-Luzzi, G. E. (1977). "Ritual as Language: The Case of South Indian Food Offerings." *Current Anthropology*, 18: 507–14.

Firth, Raymond (1973). *Symbols: Public and Private*. London: Allen & Unwin.

Griswold, A. B., and Prasert Na Nagara (1979). "Epigraphic and Historical Studies, no. 22: An Inscription from Vat Hin Tan, Sukhodaya." *Journal of the Siam Society*, 67: 71–72.

Hare, E. M., trans. (1973). *Anguttara Nikāya*. Pali Text Society. London: Routledge & Kegan Paul.

Horner, I. B., trans. (1970). *Majjhima Nikāya*, vol. 2. Pali Text Society. London: Luzac.

Kirsch, A. T. (1975). "Economy, Polity, and Religion in Thailand." In *Change and Persistence in Thai Society*, G. W. Skinner and A. T. Kirsch, eds. Ithaca, N.Y.: Cornell University Press.

Lehman, F. K. (1972). "Doctrine, Practice and Belief in Theravada Buddhism." Review of M. E. Spiro, *Buddhism and Society. Journal of Asian Studies*, 31: 373–80.

Leoffler, Lorenz (1968). "Beast, Bird, and Fish: An Essay in Southeast Asian Symbolism." In *Folk Religion and World View in the Southwestern Pacific*. Tokyo: Keio Institute of Cultural and Linguistic Studies.

Marriott, McKim (1964). "Caste Ranking and Food Transactions: A Matrix Analysis." In *Structure and Change in Indian Society*, M. Singer and B. Cohn, eds. Viking Fund Publications in Anthropology 47: 144–71.

Mus, Paul (1978). *Borobadur*. New York: Arno.

Nanomoli, Ven Thera, trans. (1966). *The Patimokkha*. Bangkok: Social Science Association Press.

Ortner, S. (1975). "Gods' Bodies, Gods' Food: A Symbolic Analysis of a Sherpa Ritual." In *The Interpretation of Symbolism*, Roy Willis, ed. New York: Wiley.

Quaritch Wales, H. G. (1931). *Siamese State Ceremonies*. London: Bernard Quaritch.

Rhys-Davids, Mrs. T. W., trans. (1971). *Sangutta Nikāya*. Pali Text Society. London: Luzac.

Sperber, Dan (1975). *Rethinking Symbolism*. Cambridge: Cambridge University Press.

Spiro, Melford (1966). "Buddhism and Economic Action in Burma." *American Anthropologist*, 68: 1163–1173.

——— (1970). *Buddhism and Society*. New York: Harper & Row.

Tambiah, S. J. (1969). "Animals Are Good to Think and Good to Prohibit." *Ethnology*, 7: 423–59.

——— (1970). *Buddhism and the Spirit Cults in North-East Thailand*. Cambridge: Cambridge University Press.

——— (1976). *World Conqueror and World Renouncer*. Cambridge: Cambridge University Press.

Terweil, B. J. (1975). *Monks and Magic*. Scandinavian Institute of Asian Studies, Monograph 24. London: Curzon.

Van Esterik, John (1977). "Cultural Interpretation of Canonical Paradox: Lay Meditation in a Central Thai Village." Ph.D. diss., University of Illinois.

Van Esterik, Penny (1982). "Interpreting a Cosmology: Guardian Spirits in Thai Buddhism."
    Anthropos, 77: 1–15.
Warren, Henry (1969). *Buddhism in Translations*. New York: Atheneum.
Woodward, F. L., trans. (1954). *Sangutta Nikāya*. vol. 3. Pali Text Society. London: Luzac.
────── (1972). *Anguttara Nikāya*, vol. 5. Pali Text Society. London: Luzac.
────── (1973). *Anguttara Nikāya*. Pali Text Society. London: Routledge & Kegan Paul.
Yalman, Nur (1969). "On the Meaning of Food Offerings in Ceylon." In *Forms of Symbolic
    Action*, R. Spencer, ed. Seattle: University of Washington Press, pp. 81–96.

AN ANTHROPOLOGICAL VIEW OF WESTERN WOMEN'S PRODIGIOUS FASTING: A REVIEW ESSAY

Carole M. Counihan

Rudolph M. Bell (1985). *Holy Anorexia.* Epilogue by William N. Davis. Chicago: University of Chicago Press.

Joan Jacobs Brumberg (1988). *Fasting Girls: The Emergence of Anorexia Nervosa as a Modern Disease.* Cambridge: Harvard University Press.

Caroline Walker Bynum (1987). *Holy Feast and Holy Fast: The Religious Significance of Food to Medieval Women.* Berkeley: University of California Press.

In prodigious fasting, sometimes to death, Western women have expressed an extraordinary relationship to food for almost eight centuries. This essay attempts to explain such behavior by weaving together the fine-grained and fascinating historical data presented in the three books under review and viewing them from the cross-cultural and holistic perspectives fundamental to anthropology. I aim to show that Western female fasting differs radically from other kinds of fasting observed by anthropologists across the globe, and that it involves a highly symbolic alteration of women's universal relationship to food. I argue that it is best understood as a multi-determined behavior, an interplay of ideological, economic, political, and social factors. Although Western culture has changed greatly over the eight centuries that women have refused food, certain forces persist, making radical fasting a significant statement. These forces include the identi-fication of women with food, a dualistic and absolutist Judeo-Christian

ideology, a patriarchal political and economic structure, and a family organization that limits female autonomy and potential.

The three books under review provide complementary data and interpretation that together illuminate the puzzle of fasting women. Rudolph
Bell contributes a psychoanalytical approach and rich, in-depth case material on several Italian holy women who, between 1200 and the present,
practiced extreme fasting. Where sources are available, he focuses on the
saints' family lives, on childhood and breastfeeding experiences, and on
evidence of the women's oral fixation. His illumination of the holy anorexics' individual psychology and family experiences provides an essential
part of the explanation of why women fast.

Caroline Walker Bynum uses a "functionalist and a phenomenological"
(p. 6) approach to focus on the cultural and symbolic dimensions of fasting. She aims "to show the manifold meanings of food and its perva-
siveness in religious symbolism" (p. 5) for medieval women. Although
she discusses hagiographers' descriptions of her subjects, she pays particular attention to the words of the saints themselves, convinced that they
reveal the richness and complexity of the fasting, eucharistic devotion,
food miracles, food donations, and miraculous bodily emissions central to
the religious expression of medieval female saints. Her book is richly
documented with the saints' poetic, erotic, ecstatic, and symbolic statements about union with God through food and fasting. It makes a crucial
contribution to the interpretation of their behavior and enables us to examine the role of ideology over time as a meaningful context for fasting.

Joan Jacobs Brumberg's book has the broadest historical and explana-
tory focus as she sets out to explain "the emergence of anorexia nervosa as
a modern disease" by considering changes in female fasting and responses
to it from the Middle Ages to the present. She uses rich primary source
material from medical journals, newspapers, and unpublished case records
on the "miraculous fasting maidens" of the 16th and 17th centuries, the
"fasting girls" of the 18th century, and especially the anorexics of the 19th
century. Brumberg concentrates on how anorexia lost its primarily spiritual dimension and became, during the Victorian era, firmly established
as a disease. She shows how "love and work in the bourgeois family"
(p. 126) incited 19th-century adolescent girls to refuse food, and she
adeptly documents how female fasting in the present day is related
to beliefs about thinness and perfection, to the subordinate position
of women in society, and to family relations. She advocates a "multi-
casual model" that considers anorexia nervosa an "addiction to starvation" triggered and supported by biological, psychological, and cultural
factors.[1]

ANTHROPOLOGY: HOLISTIC AND COMPARATIVE

A holistic concept of culture is central to anthropological method and interpretation. Culture, to quote the venerable Edward Tylor (1958: 1:1), "is that complex whole which includes knowledge, belief, art, morals, law, custom, and any other capabilities and habits acquired by man as a member of society." Anthropologists believe that any cultural artifact—whether object, behavior, symbol, or thought—must always be viewed as performed by a biological, psychological, and social human being and explained as part of a whole cultural system consisting of economy, political organization, social structure, and ideology. These components, separated for analytical simplicity, are embedded like Russian dolls. A fundamental belief of anthropology is the functional unity of cultural systems (see e.g. Geertz 1973; Wolf 1974; Peacock 1986).

An anthropological explanation of Western women's fasting begins, then, with the assumption that fasting is a piece in a cultural mosaic, an extraordinary piece but one that fits, nonetheless.[2] It can be understood only in relation to the rest of a cultural picture that includes production, distribution, consumption, resource control and allocation, power structures, public decision-making, family organization, marriage patterns, child-rearing, and belief systems, especially as these are manifest through the culture's foodways (see e.g. Richards 1939; Kahn 1986).

The cross-cultural approach, fundamental to anthropological epistemology, can also contribute to understanding of the prodigious fasting of women from the Middle Ages to the present in Europe and North America. It enables us to know how unusual or common such behavior is worldwide and to examine the conditions that incite or deter fasting to death. The comparative view enables us to see the common threads in the diversity of Western female fasting and its radical differences from the ways in which women in non-Western cultures relate to food.

The Gift and its Refusal

Food refusal, I argue, is a meaningful statement in all cultures and signifies denial of relationship. In his classic study *The Gift*, Marcel Mauss (1967) showed how culture is a system of functional unity where exchange plays a key role in linking people together, maintaining the peace, and affirming beliefs.[3] He argues that prestations are one of a number of "*total* social phenomena. In ... them, all kinds of institutions find simultaneous expression: religious, legal, moral, and economic" (p. 1). The gift involves a tripartite obligation: to give, to receive, and to repay.

Refusal to give or receive is a vast insult that severs relationships. Refusal to repay signifies inability to do so and loss of face. Giving to others is the basis of power, for recipients are beholden to donors.

Mauss considers all kinds of giving and receiving, but many of his examples involve gifts of food, which are primary among primitives and important in all societies. Marshall Sahlins (1972: 215–16) underscores the particularly strong pressures in social groups toward food-sharing and its power to determine sociability:

> Food is life-giving, urgent, ordinarily symbolic of hearth and home, if not of mother. By comparison with other stuff, food is more readily, or more necessarily, shared.... Food dealings are a delicate barometer, a ritual statement as it were, of social relations, and food is thus employed instrumentally as a starting, a sustaining, or a destroying mechanism of sociability.... Food offered in a generalized way, notably as hospitality, is good relations ... food not offered on the suitable occasion or not taken is bad relations.... In these principles of instrumental food exchange there seems little variation between peoples.

Groups as diverse as the hunting-gathering San of southern Africa (Lee 1979, 1984; Marshall 1976; Shostak 1981; Thomas 1959), the Sharanahua Indians of the Peruvian Amazon (Siskind 1973), and rural Sardinians (Counihan 1984) make food-sharing the definition of relation. Commensality—the sharing of food—establishes communion and connection in all cultures. Self-denial of food and refusal to eat with others represent a severe rupture of connection. Although the three authors differ on how similar they think female fasting is over time, and Bynum (p. 206) is right that specific meanings for food come from and vary across cultures, the ethnographic data suggest that on the most general level food refusal universally signifies rupture of connection and that this meaning is expressed by prodigious female fasters.

Women and Food

The ethnographic data suggest another universal of relevance to holy and modern anorexia: the deep connection between women and food. Food is a particularly important concern and symbol for females in all cultures (Counihan 1988). Women have universal responsibility for food preparation and consumption (D'Andrade 1974) and in many cultures for production and distribution as well (see e.g. Lee 1979). They are defined as nurtures and carry out this role principally through feeding. In addition, women themselves *are* food for their children during pregnancy and lactation, intensifying their identification with food and its relevance as symbol.

In many cultures, as among ancient and modern Aztecs in Mexico (Taggart 1983), women are associated with the fertility of the earth and its bounty.

Western women also use food as symbol of self, but the prodigious fasters base their identification with food on negation and obsession. The preponderance of fasters throughout Western history has always been female. Although men also fasted in the Middle Ages, Bynum (chap. 3) makes clear they did so with neither the prevalence nor the rigor of women who persistently "used bread, blood, hunger and eating as their dominant images for union with God and neighbor" (p. 93). Throughout the 17th, 18th, and 19th centuries, those who abstained from food relentlessly and totally were "miraculous fasting maidens" (Brumberg, p. 49) and "fasting girls" (chap. 3); "there were, in fact, no 'fasting boys'" (p. 99). Only rarely did men practice extreme fasting, and they did so to prove a specific point, like the eclectic physician Henry S. Tanner who rented Clarendon Hall in New York and fasted for forty days to show it could be done (pp. 89–90). Today, most researchers estimate that about nine out of every ten anorexics are women and conclude that the disorder is a female one, suffered by some men who share certain aspects of the feminine experience (Lawrence 1984: 13).

Obsession characterizes the identification of female fasters with food throughout Western history. For example, of the medieval saint Colomba da Rieti (b. 1497) her friends said:

> [We] never saw her taste bread, or fish, or eggs, or cheese or anything similar, nor any other food except that on some evenings she would taste a piece of fruit, sort of licking it to draw out the juice, and she drank water... sometimes she would sip a bit of chick-pea soup remaining in the nuns' bowls or suck on (but not eat) leftover salad leaves... this she did to punish her senses because the food had spoiled and was covered with flies. (Quoted in Bell, p. 156)

Other medieval holy women had tortured dreams full of food temptations, used imagery of food as God and God as food, and had an ecstatic relationship with the Eucharist. Although we lack data on the thoughts and feelings toward food of the fasting girls of the 17th, 18th and 19th centuries (Brumberg, p. 165), Colomba prefigures modern anorexics who are endlessly preoccupied with food. As Aimee Liu (1979: 153–54) says in her autobiographical account of anorexia nervosa, "Food. That's the scourge. I can't get away from it. If I don't eat I gloat, but think constantly of what I'm missing. If I do eat, I damn myself, and over and over again count up all that I regret eating. But the thing that's truly unforgivable is the way it blinds me to the rest of life." Some anorexics enact secret rituals with food, like chewing every bite one hundred times (Levenkron 1978); others focus completely on one tidbit, like Hilde Bruch's patient Tania who "would eat one tiny M & M candy very slowly, just nibbling on it, and told herself that she could feel her stomach getting full" (1978: 91).

From the 13th century to the present, food has provided an important channel for female self-expression, although its specific meanings vary. Medieval women, Bynum tells us, were culturally defined as nurturers (p. 277) and found a source of holiness in seeing themselves as food, for they identified with Christ who becomes food in the Mass to redeem humanity. Their own ability to nurse paralleled their association of "the breasts of Mary with eucharistic feeding of the soul" (p. 271). In the Victorian era, bourgeois women used elaborate food preparation and consumption as a symbol of their social position and of the love they offered their families (Brumberg, chap. 5). Modern women, particularly those with anorexia nervosa, make food and its denial in pursuit of extreme thinness the central focus of their identity, "an important analogue of the self" (p. 260).

There are major differences in what food meant for women in different historical periods, differences that parallel the overall secularization noted by both Bell (pp. 170–77) and Brumberg (p. 4 and passim) and reflect the radically different attitudes toward life and nature noted by Bynum (p. 300). Modern women seek mastery of their bodies to achieve perfection through thinness; medieval women sought transcendence of their bodies to achieve holiness through asceticism; Victorian women sought a sublime and delicate femininity through denial of bodily needs. What all these meanings have in common is negation: of the body, of female physicality, and in extreme cases of life itself.

Medieval female saints made food a central vehicle of their quest for piety. Bynum (p. 186) interprets their behavior thus:

> Women fast—and hunger becomes an image for excruciating, never-satiated love of God. Women feed—and their bodies become an image of suffering poured out for others. Women eat—and whether they devour the filth of sick bodies or the blood and flesh of the Eucharist, the foods are Christ's suffering and Christ's humanity, with which one must join before approaching triumph, glory or divinity.

Their extraordinary behaviors included not only fasting but, as Bynum emphasizes (p. 93, chaps. 4 and 5, and passim), a host of other food-centered activities. Medieval holy women cured the sick with oil or milk flowing from their bodies, before or after death. Some multiplied food in miracles, emulating Christ's miracle of the loaves and fishes. Many gave food away to the poor, often against the wishes of their fathers or husbands. Some chewed and spit out food or vomited meals they were forced to consume, like today's bulimics or bulimarexics (Boskind-White and White 1983; Cauwels 1983; Striegel-Moore, Silberstein, and Rodin 1986). Other holy fasters ate only the Eucharist, saw visions in the Eucharist or after consuming it, tasted the Host as inebriating or sweet, and could tell the consecrated from the unconsecrated Host (vomiting the latter). Some—like Saint Veronica (Bell, pp. 76–77), Catherine of Siena (Bynum, p. 172, Bell, p. 25), Catherine of Genoa (Bynum, p. 182), and Angela da Foligno (Bell, p. 108)—ate filth as sacrifice and self-abnegation: pus, scabs, lice, leprous water, rotten and bad food, cat vomit, insects, worms, and spiders. Many of their actions involved distortions of women's usual relationship to food: they bestowed their effluvia not as physical substance to their infants but as spiritual nourishment to the poor; they did not incorporate food but vomited it; they ate not food but its opposite, filth or Spirit.

Modern anorexics also have a distorted relationship to eating; they strive not for holiness, however, but for thinness and self-control through food denial (Bruch 1978: xi).[4] Anorexic girls feel great pride in their cachexia and suffer a severely disturbed body image: they cannot see their own emaciation and continually feel fat even as they starve to death. They undergo loss of over 25 percent of body weight, severe wasting, and many related health effects of starvation. They are obsessed with food and their bodies, devote themselves fanatically to dieting and exercise, and, like their medieval counterparts, convince themselves that hunger is pleasurable and valuable (Bruch 1973: chap. 14; 1978). Modern anorexics do not ordinarily seek religious transcendence and union with God through fasting,[5] though many report the experience makes them feel clean, pure, and good (Bruch 1978: 18). Liu (1979: 109) exemplifies this: "Dieting, as far as I was concerned, was like a contest between good (abstinence) and evil (indulgence). If I followed through with the game, I'd purify myself. As long as I continued to eat in my wanton manner, I was tainted." Food is transformed from a path to physical sustenance into a vehicle for morality.

Holy and modern anorexics have a distorted relationship to food. Rather than focus primarily on nurturing others, they concentrate on denying self. Food no longer serves primarily to connect them to others but rather to enable them to transcend their mundane and earthly selves in the quest for piety or perfection.

Fasting in Cross-Cultural Perspective

"Holy anorexics," "fasting girls," and modern anorexics share further characteristics that appear in clear relief when contrasted to fasting by other, non-Western, nonstratified peoples (Powdermaker 1960). Such differences provide a key to understanding Western women and the meaning of their food use. In all cultures, food is an important symbol; however, the meanings attributed to food and the way in which it is manipulated to convey messages vary widely across cultures (see e.g. Barthes 1975; Douglas 1972, 1984; Kahn 1986; Lévi-Strauss 1969; Meigs 1984; Tambiah 1969; Verdier 1969; Weismantel 1988). Mary Douglas (1973) asserts that "the human body is always treated as an image of society" (p. 70) and that the passage of food in and out of the body can stand for social boundaries and their transgression. Most important for our concerns here is her claim that "bodily control is an expression of social control" (1973: 70). Western women's strong concern to control their food intake is a metaphor for their efforts to control their own bodies and destinies in a culture that makes self-control a moral imperative; this, however, reveals prevalent Western concerns and is not a cultural universal.

Many non-Western peoples practice fasting,[6] but rarely with the totality or relentlessness of Western fasting women (see Katona-Apte 1975: 317–21, Messer 1989). "Abstinence is followed by indulgence" (Goody 1982: 78), and feasts regularly interrupt periods of reduced consumption, as in the harvest festivals that follow the annual lean times among the Gonja of northern Ghana. Muslims, for example, break the daily fast during Ramadan each night with hearty eating (Messina 1988). Anorexia nervosa and mirabilis are, by contrast, endless.

In tribal societies fasting is ordinarily collective and ritualized. A social group or the whole of a society will avoid certain foods; their fasting will follow traditional forms, be endowed with specific meanings, and be sanctioned by society. The LoDagaa of northern Ghana hold an annual Bagre ceremony (Goody 1982: chap. 3) where a series of food prohibitions is laid on initiands and then gradually lifted over a period of several weeks. The "cancellation of the prohibitions takes the form of a public demonstration" (p. 81) where initiated boys eat foods previously forbidden. Their temporary and partial fasting is followed by a public feast and is imbued with significance through collective celebration. Both feasting and fasting—through the ability to control appetite, defer consumption, and share food—affirm humanity and sociability. By contrast, the Western fasting we are considering is solitary, sometimes secretive, and not publicly ritualized.

Fasts by non-Western peoples most commonly "demand an alternative diet rather than total denial" (Goody 1982: 117). The Kalaunans of Goodenough Island eat "hard, dry foods ... to fill the belly and satisfy the appetite for long periods" rather than "soft, pulpy food" (Young 1986: 117). The Trobriand Islanders perform *vilamalya* magic to make their cultivated food last a long time by making them "inclined to eat wild fruit of the bush" (Malinowski 1922: 169). Boys undergoing initiation among the Hua of New Guinea (Meigs 1984: chap. 2) are enjoined from eating certain foods associated with females because these are believed dangerous, but they are simultaneously encouraged to eat a host of foods believed to fortify and protect them. Even in medieval Western Christendom, the norm was limited fasts on Fridays, holy days, and during Lent, when meat and rich foods were spurned but simple foods such as bread, fish, water, and greens were allowed (Bynum, p. 40). In fact, as Bynum (p. 47) and Bell (pp. 118ff.) note, total fasting was condemned by the Church, and many of the holy anorexics faced staunch opposition from church authorities—opposition they steadily circumvented with claims they were unable to counter God's will by eating.

In spite of ecclesiastical, medical, and social opposition, Western women have fasted to death since at least the 13th century. Whereas in tribal cultures people never (to my knowledge) die of voluntary starvation, an estimated 15–19 percent of severe anorexics die (Brumberg, p. 13; Gordon 1988). Brumberg documents case after case of 17th, 18th, and 19th-century girls who died from their refusal to eat. Many of the holy fasters explicitly wished for death, among them Margaret of Cortona, who said to her confessor after he urged her to eat, "Dear Father, I have no intention of making a peace pact between my body and my soul, and neither do I intend to hold back. Therefore allow me to tame my body by not altering my diet; I will not stop for the rest of my life until there is no life left" (quoted in Bell, p. 101).

Western women's fasting is antisocial, endless, total, and deadly; it is unlike what people in most other societies practice. Perhaps there are shared characteristics over time of the cultural milieus in which women find inedia a meaningful activity which explain why a significant number have fasted to death. I consider here the causal significance of ideology, patriarchal and stratified political and economic structure, and family organization. These factors are partially described in the books under review, which give some data on historical differences, but systematic consideration of their interrelation and similarity over time can illuminate Western women's food refusal.

IDEOLOGY

Absolutism and the Quest for Perfection

Western women's fasting has manifestly different goals in different historical periods. These differences are related to the overall process of secularization

(Bell, pp. 170–77; Brumberg, passim) and to significant differences in culture. Yet even as the West has become manifestly less religious, certain ideological tenets have persisted because they are deeply ingrained in Western culture. The Judeo-Christian ideology—unlike that of many other societies—is both dualistic and absolutist, based on "a dichotomy of absolute goodness and evil, absolute strength and weakness, absolute truth and absolute untruth":

> The Judeo-Christian orientation contrasts sin and virtue, grace and non-grace, fall and redemption in order to comprehend the role of the divine in sustaining goodness, virtue and so on. Within the general schema of Judeo-Christian thought it is necessary to have diametrically opposed contrasts, and within the lives of individuals a person judges the virtuousness of his present life, achieved through the grace of God, with his sinful past. (Pandian 1985: 50)

During the Middle Ages, Jacob Pandian (1985: 51) notes, Western culture lost the "conceptual package of the vast range of human possibility and self identity" that had been presented in Greek mythology, with its array of gods—jealous, wise, silly, angry, composed, weak, powerful, and so on. What remained was perfection simply and radically contrasted with perdition.

Medieval women strive for holiness through fasting, Victorian girls seek the wasting and weakness associated with social and spiritual superiority, and modern women strive for thinness, but all are seeking perfection in the value system of their culture. William Davis (1985: 181–82) suggests that "both [thinness and holiness] represent ideal states of being in the cultural milieus under consideration." Brumberg (p. 7) says, "anorexia nervosa appears to be a secular addiction to a new kind of perfectionism, one that links personal salvation to the achievement of an external body configuration, rather than an internal spiritual state." Thus women persistently seek to attain an absolute standard of perfection through fasting, but alter the definition of perfection as their societies become increasingly secularized.

The persistence of the absolutist ideology over time is implicated in the obsessive way in which Western women fast. Food refusal must be total; anything less fails to achieve the desired state of perfection. Although many medieval saints, like Catherine of Siena (Bell, chap. 2; Bynum, p. 169) and Margaret of Cortona (Bell, p. 101), were ordered by their confessors and religious superiors to take food, they refused in the belief that total fasting was essential to their holiness and union with God. Brumberg documents many cases of women in the 17th, 18th, and 19th centuries, like Ann Moore (p. 60) and Sarah Jacob (pp. 64ff.), who either pretended to or did refuse all food, for the impression of total fasting was integral to their self-concept and impact on others. Modern anorexics tenaciously adhere to a rigid diet and feel that any transgression undermines their quest for achievement. As Aimee Liu (1979: 40) says, "I'm becoming famous around school for my display of self-discipline... In this one respect, I'm the best, but if I let it go, all is lost, so I cling to my diet tenaciously." But total fasting is too painful and difficult for most women, and so many—perennial dieters or severe bulimics—oscillate dangerously back and forth between fasting and bingeing, overeating and purging, consumed with guilt over their failure to fast or diet perfectly.

Mind–Body Dualism and Denigration of the Female

Another persistent foundation of Western ideology, unlike that of many non-Western tribal peoples (Pandian 1985), is the dichotomy of mind and body. The literature under review on medieval (Bynum, p. 36, chap. 6; Bell, pp. 118–21), Victorian (Brumberg, p. 63), and contemporary female fasters (Brumberg, p. 243) makes clear that central issues for such women are belief in the separateness of mind and body and the moral value in dominance of body by mind (Chernin 1981). Brumberg (pp. 77ff.) tells us, for example, that the fourteen-year fast of the "Brooklyn Enigma," Mollie Fancher, was seen by her Spiritualist followers as evidence of "the duality of the mind and the body" (p. 87).

This duality has been integral to Western morality from at least the time of the ancient Greeks (Bell, pp. 118–19). The two chief ways of enacting mind's control of the body are fasting and chastity. Bynum (p. 2) argues that for medieval people, "to repress eating and hunger was to control the body in a discipline far more basic than any achieved by shedding the less frequent and essential gratifications of sex or money." For Victorians, sexuality was tightly controlled and "appetite was regarded as a barometer of sexuality" (Brumberg, p. 175); hence denial of appetite stood for suppression of sexuality. In modern society, control of food intake has assumed paramount importance in the demonstration of morality. Sexual control may have become relatively unimportant, but limitation of eating in the midst of affluence, constant availability of food, and relentless promotion of consumption through advertising is both difficult and highly revered (Brumberg, Afterword; Mackenzie 1976; Schwartz 1986).

In the Western dualistic tradition, women are identified with nature and the sensual body that must be controlled, and men are associated with culture and the mind that controls (Bynum, p. 282; Chernin 1981), as in the story of Adam, the doubting mind, tempted by Eve, the wanton flesh (see Chernin 1987). Women who seek value and worth in the definitional terms of Western culture must dominate their appetites by their wills, thus affirming their spirituality, discipline, and morality. In a culture that postulates dominance of mind over sense and associates women with the body and its appetite, the burden of control falls particularly strongly on women.

Because of women's depiction in the dichotomous worldview, their quest for perfection necessitates dominance of the body through control of food consumption and endurance of hunger. Bynum and Bell describe over and over again how medieval women tortured themselves by trying to repress their hunger in an effort to become holy. "Pain/suffering" was equated with "pleasure/love" (Bell, p. 60), and hunger stood for "hungering for God" (Bynum, p. 152). The 13th-century Flemish mystic Hadewijch, for example, wrote beautiful mystical poems expressing her belief that "hunger ... is incorporation with Christ's suffering humanity, which is our path to his divinity. The more we hunger with Christ, the more we are filled" (Bynum, p. 160). Brumberg shows how Victorian women found appetite vulgar, unfeminine, unspiritual, and immoral (chap. 7). Food was associated with lower-class status, "work and drudgery," "gluttony" and "physical ugliness" (p. 179), and appetite with "sexuality" and "a lack of self-restraint" (p. 178). Abstention from food signified social refinement, delicacy, daintiness, and morality—those characteristics most admired by Victorian women. Similarly, anorexics, like Aimee Lie (1979: 40), define their self-worth in terms of the self-discipline they muster to limit consumption.

While affirming the importance of mind–body dualism as a meaningful context for holy women's fasting, Bynum claims that medieval women were not merely expressing an internalized cultural misogyny based on "masochism or dualism" (p. 208). Rather, unlike modern anorexics, they were seizing power and making a positive statement with their fasting. She argues, in fact, that one of the lessons of the Middle Ages for moderns is that:

> Medieval people saw food and body as sources of life, repositories of sensation. Thus food and body signified generativity and suffering. Food which must be destroyed in order to give life, and body, which must be torn in order to give birth, became synonymous; in identifying themselves with both, women managed to give meaning to a physical, human existence in which suffering was unavoidable ....
>
> In contrast, modern people see food and body as resources to be controlled. Thus food and body signify that which threatens human mastery.... Body and food are thus symbols of the failure of our efforts to control ourselves. (p. 300)

Bynum underscores an important difference in medieval and modern attitudes toward suffering. In the Middle Ages, women reveled in bodily agony, which they saw as redemptive; although the body could be a source of evil, its suffering could also bring salvation. Victorian women viewed suffering with some reverence as a path to bodily delicacy (Brumberg, chap. 5). Modern women attempt to negate the body and its pain, which represent failure of the mind's ability to control the senses. In spite of this difference, fasting women share a belief in the body as potential source of evil and a fear of their own susceptibility to temptation. Although Lois Paul (1974) reports a similar belief for Mayan Indian women (heavily influenced by Christianity), and many cultures define the female body as polluting (Douglas 1966; Meigs 1984; Delaney, Lupton and Toth 1988), I know of no culture where women attempt to purify their bodies with the total and inexorable food refusal that characterizes holy, Victorian, and modern anorexics.

Denial of Female Sexuality and Reproduction

Across time a shared characteristic of Western women who fast excessively is the denial of their reproductive potential and their sexuality. This, I believe, stems from the ambivalent attitude of Judeo-Christians toward the body, simultaneously a source of life and of temptation. All starving women, including medieval (Bynum, pp. 138, 148, 214, 217), Victorian (Brumberg, p. 132), and modern (Bruch 1973: 275) fasters, stop menstruating and their feminine curves disappear. A starving person loses all sexual desire (Firth 1959; Holmberg 1969; Turnbull 1972; Winnick 1979). As Margaret Mead noted (1967: 144), for women both eating and sexual intercourse involve "inception"; cessation of eating can stand for denial of all inception, including the sexual. Appetite and the "sexual instinct," the mouth and the vagina, are symbolically connected (Freud 1962: 1); closing the mouth to food stands for closing the vagina to sex.

Fear of, disgust with, and refusal of sexual connection are common themes in the worldviews of anorexics and medieval saints and are linked to their food refusal. Although explicit discussions of sex are rare among late 19th-century anorexics, there is evidence that "confused or unfulfilled expectation in the domain of courtship was a common precipitating agent in the mental disorders of adolescent girls" (Brumberg, pp. 134–35). Numerous studies (Orbach 1978; Millman 1980: 188–89; Chernin 1981; Bruch 1973: 275–80) of contemporary women with eating disorders report their hostility toward sexual contact with men. Aimee Liu (1979: 101), for example, says, "God, how I hated men! They made my skin crawl. Worse, they made me despise myself, my body, my sex. They were bastards, it was true, but mine was the flesh that teased them. Ugh, what an abominable business. There had to be a way out, to become androgynous." And so she stopped eating, delighted in the disappearance of menses and breasts, and wished to crawl "back into the body of a child" (p. 41). Her attitude is similar to that of the 14th-century Dominican nun Francesca Bussa, who refused food as part of her total horror of sex:

> The consummation of the marriage, when she was but thirteen, had an immediate and traumatic effect on the girl; no sooner had the wedding celebration ended, than without warning she suddenly lost all her strength, became paralyzed and dumb, and she was totally unable to eat.... By the age of seventeen or eighteen Francesca had reduced her food intake to only one meal each day, and this one spartan in the extreme: no fish, eggs, chicken, or anything sweet or delicate, only bitter legumes and beans not even flavored with oil.... She slept only two hours each day, and even during these times she told of being tortured by dreams of men who carried giant cooked onions (a food she detested and that always nauseated her) and smeared them over her face and stuffed them in her mouth. (Bell, pp. 136–38)

The absolutism, dualism, and diffidence toward female sexuality characteristic of Judeo-Christian ideology provide a context for women who evince strong ambivalence toward their sensual appetites. They deny them but are tormented by thoughts of food or by sexual demons. They attempt to quench their desires, but constant self-denial only exacerbates them. Negation of bodily appetite unites Western fasting women and provides a path to individual autonomy and achievement where few other such paths exist.

PATRIARCHY AND FEMALE SUBORDINATION

The holistic and comparative perspective can illuminate how Western women's fasting relates to their historically evolving, subordinate social and economic position, which limits channels to their self-expression. The three books under review all raise and treat in different ways the question whether women's prodigious fasting is a response to and struggle against patriarchy.[7] To a certain extent they, like many contemporary works on anorexia nervosa (see Counihan 1985), believe it is. Although the books present important insights related to this question, none offers an explicit definition of patriarchy and a clear exposition of how women's fasting protests against it.

From an anthropological perspective, a patriarchy is a society where women are politically, economically, socially, and ideologically devalued and disadvantaged, where they lack control of economic resources and power, and where they are deemed morally and physically inferior to men.

Systematic analysis of the fasting women's specific place in a system of class and gender inequality is lacking in the three books.[8] Western society has changed enormously from the Middle Ages to the present, of course, but over time women have had a particularly powerless, secondary, and mute position when compared to women in nonhierarchical, non-Western societies.

Anthropologists (e.g. Brown 1975; Lee 1979; Murphy and Murphy 1985; Shostak 1981;Weiner 1988) have documented case after case of nonstratified societies where women have much influence, through their control over resources and their important role in food production and distribution as well as in its preparation and consumption. Women among the Iroquois (Brown 1975), for example, possessed considerable power because they produced the most important foods—corn, beans, and squashes, the "three sisters"—and because they controlled distribution, which was a main channel for creating obligations in others. Iroquois women also held the stores of food (a main source of wealth) and used that control to influence political decisions.

But unlike their tribal sisters, Western women who practice prodigious fasting do not control important economic resources, work actively in production, or manage distribution; they administer only food preparation and consumption, largely within the home. Although Bell (e.g. p. 88) and particularly Bynum (chap. 7) mention how medieval women circumvented male authority by distributing food to the poor, this was not their legitimate purview and it incited opprobrium from fathers, husbands, and religious authorities. Control of consumption is Western women's principal channel for expression of identity, influence, and will (Counihan 1988). Refusal of food produced and given by others is, as we discussed above in reference to Mauss, a refusal to be beholden. Fasting is one of the few legitimate ways for women to exert control without overtly challenging male power—perhaps why they are obsessed with food and fasting in a way non-Western women, who have other channels for influence, are not.

FAMILY, FASTING, AUTONOMY, AND RELATIONSHIPS

Patriarchal Western society not only restricts women's economic and political opportunities but also defines their role within the family as nurturer and food provider, a role compatible with the use of food as voice. Although most women in Western society have been relatively powerless, only a few have chosen prodigious fasting. These are women who, because of specific family experiences, may have had particularly severe psychological difficulties with autonomy, intimacy, and eating.

Researchers of contemporary anorexia nervosa (e.g. Bruch 1973, 1978; Lawrence 1984; Minuchin, Rosman and Baker 1978) have suggested that anorexia is related to specific family dynamics. In particular, eating disorders arise in families where parents are concerned with perfection and are overinvolved with, overidentified with, and overprotective of their children, restricting their independence and autonomy. Furthermore, eating disorders are likely to arise in families where parents confuse food with love and fail to respond appropriately to children's needs, interfering with their ability to recognize hunger and satiety and to use food appropriately (Bruch 1973: chap. 4). Some parents are themselves overly concerned about the relationship between food, the body, and self-worth—they see food consumption primarily as the path to moral rectitude. How such family patterns are implicated in modern eating disorders is well-established, but because of an absence of data it is less clear whether similar patterns existed in past cases of female fasters. However, what information is available on the family relationships of medieval and Victorian fasters is suggestive.

Food refusal, we noted above, is denial of relation, and fasting to death is the ultimate rupture of human connection. Difficulty with intimacy and relationship is a clear theme in all Western female fasting, which is self-absorbed and narcissistic. Medieval holy woman turned inward to search for God in themselves; as Catherine of Genoa wrote, "My *ME* is God" (Bynum, p. 277). Modern anorexics become totally self-involved; as Aimee Liu (1979: 75) writes, "The mirrors, this one and another large wall mirror over the sink in the bathroom, play an important part in my life now. For hours I hold court through them with myself." Medieval, Victorian, and modern fasters have solitary lives and few friends; in fact, adherence to the fast and the ascetic routine involve hours of reclusion each day, leaving little time for relations with others.

In his epilogue to Bell's book, William Davis offers an interesting hypothesis to explain the inward-facing stance of fasting women. He refers to Carol Gilligan's (1981) findings that female identity is based on relationships and suggests that the prodigious fasters have a particularly strong need for superhuman connection. The holy faster sought and established a *direct* union with God, unmediated by male authority. "She wanted above all to be deeply connected to just herself, independent of the needs that would inevitably bring her into a hierarchic, submissive, and 'possessed' relationship with men" (p. 184). Modern anorexics "ignore affiliation and focus instead upon acquiring power" (p. 185); they find themselves totally bereft of the sense of identity that women achieve through relationships.

Less clear is the difficulty of middle-class Victorian girls with relation-ships; perhaps the fact that their "options for self-expressions outside the family were limited by parental concern and social convention" (Brumberg, p. 188) made their relationships similarly limited.

The family is the most immediate breeding ground of the girl's inedia, and it is the domain most radically upset by her fasting. Brumberg (p. 134) aptly describes the 19th-century girl's refusal of the food gifts so funda-mental to middle-class nurturance as "a striking disfunction in the bour-geois family system." Many researchers have considered the role of family dynamics, particularly the mother–daughter relationship, in causing con-temporary anorexia nervosa. Feminists such as Susie Orbach (1978, 1982) and Kim Chernin (1981, 1985, 1987) have suggested that the mother–daughter relationship is extremely problematical in a patriarchal society where daughters identify with their mothers but cannot respect them because of their subordinate position. Mothers want their daughters to excel but inhibit their development because it would emphasize the moth-ers' own lack of achievement. Girls respond by seeking autonomy and excellence through a channel that strikes mothers literally in the gut but does not challenge their life choices.

Brumberg's discussion of "love and food in the bourgeois family" in the Victorian era (chap. 5) shows how family conflicts can result in anorexia nervosa. In this social milieu food is of central importance, daughters undergo prolonged dependence, and the family, particularly the relation-ship between mother and daughter, is increasingly oppressive. The 19th-century girl was the symbol and vehicle of maternal social striving; food represented love, social status, and proper etiquette. The Victorian girl suffocated by familial possessiveness and aspirations found a perfect form of rebellion in food refusal. This was a way of protesting the oppres-sive nature of relationships without breaking them and clearly symbolized the girl's ambivalence toward familial connections.

Some evidence suggests that medieval fasters were involved in a similar struggle with their mothers for autonomy. Mary Magdalen de' Pazzi, for example, "waged her most severe emotional battles" (Bell, p. 172) against her mother and competed with her for holiness and her father's affection. Bell (p. 32) says of Catherine of Siena, one of the most dramatic and influential holy anorexics,

In so ordinary and seemingly trivial a contest of wills as weaning, it had to be mother Lapa who triumphed over daughter Catherine, but as an adult this particular child made sure never to lose such battles, often redefining a situation in her mind so that what might appear to others as obedience in this world was to her a triumph in the next for the bridegroom with whom she was united.

In medieval, Victorian, and modern middle-class families, fasting women are those with a special need for autonomy. Often they are particularly intelligent, striving, creative, or imaginative women who feel especially fettered by the confinement of their social role. Most contemporary anorexics are high achievers, ostensibly successful in school, sports, and life until the disorder takes over (Bruch 1978: chap. 3). Many of the holy anorexics were also uncommon women: ambitious, perfectionist, articulate, poetic, capable of fanatical devotion to their religious fasting, "cheerful," "outgoing," and "boisterous" (Bell, p. 114). Although Bell (chap. 4) documents a whole group of holy anorexics who turned to their behaviors after marriage and childbirth, most medieval (Bynum, p. 119), Victorian (Brumberg, passim), and modern (Bruch 1978: chap. 4) fasters appeared to begin or to intensify their extraordinary behaviors around adolescence, a time when the mother–daughter relationship becomes particularly difficult as the daughter begins to define her adult female identity. Because of the centrality and significance of food for women and their lack of other means (Bynum, chap. 6), women use its refusal as the central vehicle in their search for identity, relationship, and autonomy.

Traumatic feeding in infancy and early childhood may explain why some women become fasters where others, facing similar cultural and psychological problems, do not. Freudian psychology, as Brumberg (p. 213) and Bell (p. 11) both discuss, turned attention to this domain. In a seminal paper, Anna Freud (1946) extended many of her father's implicit notions about the importance of feeding in establishing a child's personality, relationship to the mother, and later attitude toward food.[9] Bruch (1973: chap. 4) discovered that parental failure to teach children appropriate recognition of and response to hunger and satiety was the basis of many of her patients' eating disorders. Bell believes that patterns for future relationships are determined by the consistency or inconsistency of breast-feeding. For example, he attributes Catherine of Siena's great capacity for faith to her "oral contentment" in infancy (pp. 30–35) and Catherine of Rocconigi's psychological and spiritual turmoil to the fact that her mother lacked breastmilk and "sent the infant around in her brother Luigi's arms to beg suckle from healthier village women" (p. 159).

Anthropologists have provided data that give an interesting perspective on how traumatic early childhood feeding can affect adult personality and attitudes toward food without causing anorexia nervosa. Dorothy Shack (1969) and William Shack (1971) argue that the inconsistent feeding of infants and children among the Gurage of Ethiopia, including deprivation when hungry and forced gorging when satiated, is responsible for a host of personality traits prevalent among adult Gurage including: "selfishness," "emotional detachment," "unrelatedness," "passivity," "dependency," "feelings of worthlessness," and food anxiety (D. Shack 1969: 298). Low-status Gurage males, those most deprived of food and most subject to "dependency-frustration" by the mother, suffer *awre* spirit possession reminiscent of but markedly different from anorexia nervosa. It is characterized by "loss of appetite, nausea and intermittent attacks of severe stomach pains" (W. Shack 1971: 35). The spirit is exorcised in a collective ritual where the victim's relatives feed him special ceremonial food until the *awre* spirit cries out from inside him, "I am satisfied" (p. 36). The Gurage show that psychological disorders are expressed through eating in non-Western as well as Western societies, and that psychological disorders centered on food can indeed be determined by inappropriate infant feeding and family dynamics, but they also show that the sex of the victim and the use of food to resolve the disorder depend on the unique cultural, social, economic, and psychological setting. Data from anthropology confirm Brumberg's (p. 24) claim that "anorexia nervosa is clearly a multi-determined disorder that depends on the individual's biológic vulnerability, psychological predisposition, family, and the social climate."

CONCLUSION

The holistic and cross-cultural perspective of anthropology can help explain the prodigious fasting of Western women over eight hundred years by drawing into relief a similar, though not identical, array of cultural forces that have influenced their relationship to food and the body. An absolutist, dualistic worldview has established a context where total denial of appetite is a meaningful and admired path to perfection. Patriarchal society has relegated women to a secondary position by virtue of their sex. Some—perhaps particularly ambitious and striving women fettered by oppressive families—seek a voice and struggle against their subordination by refusing food. They choose fasting because of the Western belief that the mind should dominate the body and because of the centrality of food in their lives. It is the most important resource they control, even as they control only its consumption. Denial of food and appetite brings its practitioners moral worth, admiration, and the socially desired states of holiness, daintiness, or thinness, ephemeral states that can involve the fasters' entire negation through death.

The self-destructive relationship between Western women, the body, and food is, I contend, significantly different from that of women in many non-Western cultures, for reasons that bear continuing investigation by both historians and anthropologists. We need more data to answer the questions opened by this essay: How has the development of capitalism affected and altered women's relationship to their bodies, food, and fasting? How has the commoditization of the body, especially the female body, through fashion and art (Berger 1972; Nochlin 1988), contributed to the ideological reinforcement of female subordination and to women's alienation from their physical selves manifest in extreme inedia? Does women's relentless fasting express their efforts to become significant social *actors* in the context of the growing economic superfluousness of their labor (Quaggiotto 1989)? Do women fast to death in similar ways in cultural contexts where they are economically significant actors? How can we explain the anorexia nervosa of contemporary Japanese women noted by Gordon (1988) and Brumberg (p. 13, pp. 280–81, n.15), to what extent is it caused by "rapid Westernization" (Brumberg, p. 13) or by other indigenous cultural forces, and what light does it cast on our understanding of Western women's food refusal? Finally, how do we explain anorexia nervosa in men without invalidating claims that fasting over centuries is intimately related to the specific experience of women? Although I think some men fast for different reasons, and that these reasons need further investigation, I believe that other men become fasters because they share female subordination, the lack of meaningful outlets for self-expression, and the absolutist moral ideology that puts a premium on asceticism. I fear that as long as Western culture denies many women (and some men) opportunities for self-realization, power, and meaningful connection; as long as it encloses them in oppressive families and trivializes the figure of the mother; and as long as it insists on an absolute standard of perfection, some women will continue to turn to the sometimes fatal manipulation of their own food consumption as a means of self-definition.

ACKNOWLEDGEMENTS

For reading and commenting on this paper, I thank Steve Kaplan, Pamela Quaggiotto, and especially Jim Taggart, who read more drafts than either of us remembers.

NOTES

1. Current knowledge suggests that biological disfunction does not seem to be the cause of holy or modern anorexia (Bell, pp. 14–15; Brumberg, pp. 24–27; Bruch 1973: chap. 3). Although biological symptoms occur in medieval and modern fasters—including distorted

perception, sensitivity to cold and light, lanugo, constipation, slowed metabolism, hormone imbalance, hypothalmic disfunction, and amenorrhea (Bruch 1973; Bynum, pp. 119–48; Bell, passim)—they appear to be *effects* rather than *causes*. In studies of near and total starvation, neither anthropologists (Holmberg 1969; Turnbull 1972) nor researchers on war and concentration camp victims (Bruch 1973: chap. 2; Winnick 1979) have observed that a lack of food alone causes anorexia nervosa. Bell (p. 14) concurs for medieval people: "Starvation alone certainly did not cause holy anorexia." Furthermore, feeding does not cure the disorder; anorexics who are forcefed usually start fasting again as soon as they can (Bruch 1978: chap. 6; Lawrence 1984: chap. 5), whereas "normal" starvation victims welcome food (Firth 1959; Winnick 1979). However, some people seem to be susceptible to what Brumberg calls "an addiction to starvation"; some people—and there is no reason why they should exist only in Western society—seem to have a biological predisposition. But they will not become holy or anorexic fasters unless both cultural and psychological forces make food self-denial a powerful statement.

2. Geertz (1973: 43) affirms that "it may be in the cultural particularities of a people—in their oddities—that some of the most instructive revelations of what it is to be generally human are to be found."

3. The significance of exchange is so fundamental in anthropology as to be axiomatic. See, for example, Lévi-Strauss 1967, Malinowski 1922, and Weiner 1988.

4. There is an enormous literature on anorexia nervosa, which is well-covered in Brumberg's book, especially in chapter 1 and its notes. Feminist approaches to eating disorders are reviewed in Counihan 1985. Some important titles are Bruch 1973, 1978, 1988; Boskind-Lodhal 1976; Boskind-White and White 1983; Cauwels 1983; Chernin 1981, 1985; Dally 1969; Garfinkel and Garner 1982; Gordon 1988; Lawrence 1984; Levenkron 1982; Macleod 1981; Orbach 1978, 1982; Palazzoli 1974; and Striegel-Moore, Silberstein, and Rodin 1986.

5. The description by one of my female college students of her bout with anorexia nervosa supports claims for the cultural persistence of certain themes in extreme fasting and indicates that pursuit of religious purity and asceticism can still be a meaningful component of it: "I become a member of a holiness church .... I decided to practice aestheticism [asceticism] and suffered anorexia nervosa. All this was an attempt to control my life and please God. I would go on liquid fasts for days at a time and read the Bible for hours. If I began to have sexual desires, I went on a fast to put my body under subjection to the Bible—in short get rid of the sexual desire. The Bible encouraged presenting yourself as a living sacrifice unto God. And I did. I went overboard with my practices to achieve holiness" (journal, December 6, 1988).

6. Some well-documented examples are the Gurage of Ethiopia (D. Shack 1969; W. Shack 1971), the Kalaunans of Goodenough Island (Young 1971, 1986), the Trobriand Islanders of Melanesia (Malinowski 1922), the Siriono of Bolivia (Holmberg 1969), and the Bemba of Northern Rhodesia (Richards 1939).

7. Bell's major claim is that "a historically significant group of women exhibited an anorexic behavior pattern in response to the patriarchal social structures in which they were trapped" (p. xii). Medieval holy women, he claims, struggled against their subordinate social position by exerting their will to fast to circumvent male authority and establish a direct connection to God. Bynum (p. 295) differs from Bell in claiming that medieval holy women are not best viewed as victims of patriarchy. Although male hagiographers depicted them thus, Bynum (p. 208) asserts they were seizing power and establishing a direct connection to God through fasting, not just reacting against male dominance. Brumberg does not explicitly characterize women's fasting as a reaction against patriarchy, for she emphasizes its diverse aims and meanings over time, and desires not to reduce an array of female behaviors to opposition to men (p. 37). However, her book documents the clear relations of dominance-subordination between male interpreters of fasting and female practitioners. Furthermore, her proposals for reducing the incidence of contemporary anorexia involve giving women a sense of the value of their sex and

support for "their specific aspirations [and] for female creativity in general" (p. 269), implying that their self-destructive fasting is related to their subordination.

8. Some of the holy fasters were of urban, well-off families (Bynum, p. 18). Modern anorexics are predominantly of upper-middle-class, white families or of upwardly mobile, lower-middle-class families (Bruch 1978; Lawrence 1984), with an incidence of around one case per hundred thousand Americans and somewhere between one and twenty severe cases per hundred female college and high school students (Brumberg, p. 13). Anorexia nervosa and bulimia are relatively rare among black girls in the United States and Western Europe (Brumberg, p. 280, n. 14). It has been suggested that black women achieve noticeably more respect and status than white women within the family and community and that control of food exchanges is an important source of their power (Stack 1974; Styles 1980). A number of Brumberg's examples were middle-class, like Mollie Fancher, of a "moderately circumstanced, respectable, intelligent and well connected family" (*Brooklyn Daily Eagle*, June 7, 1866, quoted in Brumberg, p. 79). Others, however, were of "humble" (p. 47) origin: Ann Moore was the "daughter of a laborer" (p. 56), and Sarah Jacob was "one of seven children of... crofters" in rural Wales (p. 64). In fact, Brumberg says, "late-nineteenth-century fasting girls were generally not the daughters of the urban, educated, or secularly minded bourgeoisie" (p. 91). Rather, they were the last relics of "an older female religious culture" (p. 100). More data on the fasters are needed to test Pamela Quaggiotto's (1989) suggestion that perhaps women chose to fast to reaffirm themselves as actors, a role denied them when their labor became superfluous.

9. Anna Freud (1946: 126) believes that the child's "conflicting behavior towards food" stems from "conflicting emotions towards the mother which are transferred on to the food which is a symbol for her. Ambivalence towards the mother may express itself as fluctuations between over-eating and refusal of food; guilty feelings towards the mother and a consequent inability to enjoy her affection as an inability to enjoy food; obstinacy and hostility towards the mother as a struggle against being fed."

REFERENCES

Barthes, Roland (1975 [orig. 1961]). "Toward a Psychosociology of Contemporary Food Consumption." *European Diet from Pre-Industrial to Modern Times*, ed. Elborg Foster and Robert Foster, pp. 47–59. New York: Harper & Row.

Berger, John (1972). *Ways of Seeing*. New York: Penguin.

Boskind-Lodahl, Marlene (1976). "Cinderella's Stepsisters: A Feminist Perspective on Anorexia Nervosa and Bulimia." *Signs* 2, 342–56.

Boskind-White, Marlene, and William C. White (1983). *Bulimarexia: The Binge/Purge Cycle*. New York: Norton.

Brown, Judith K. (1975). "Iroquois Women: An Ethnohistorical Note." In *Toward an Anthropology of Women*, ed. Rayna R. Reiter, pp. 235–51. New York: Monthly Review.

Bruch, Hilde (1973). *Eating Disorders: Obesity, Anorexia Nervosa, and the Person Within*. New York: Basic Books.

Bruch, Hilde (1978). The Golden Cage: *The Enigma of Anorexia Nervosa*. New York: Vintage.

Bruch, Hilde (1988). *Conversations with Anorexics*. Ed. Danita Czyzewski and Melanie Suhr. New York: Basic Books.

Cauwels, Janice M. (1983). *Bulimia: The Binge-Burge Compulsion*. Garden City, N. Y.: Doubleday.

Chernin, Kim (1981). *The Obsession: Reflections on the Tyranny of Slenderness*. New York: Harper & Row.

Chernin, Kim (1985). *The Hungry Self*. New York: Times Books.

Chernin, Kim (1987). *Reinventing Eve: Modern Woman in Search of Herself*. New York: Times Books.

Counihan, Carole (1984). "Bread as World: Food Habits and Social Relations in Modernizing Sardinia." *Anthropological Quarterly* 57 (2), 47–59.

Counihan, Carole (1985). "What Does It Mean To Be Fat, Thin, and Female in the United States?" *Food and Foodways* 1 (1), 77–94.

Counihan, Carole (1988). "Female Identity, Food and Power in Contemporary Florence." *Anthropological Quarterly* 61 (2), 51–62.

Dally, Peter (1969). *Anorexia Nervosa*. New York: Grune & Stratton.

D'Andrade, Roy (1974). "Sex Differences and Cultural Institutions." In *Culture and Personality: Contemporary Readings*, ed. Robert A. Levine, pp. 16–39. New York: Aldine.

Davis, William N. (1985). "Epilogue." In *Holy Anorexia* by Rudolph M. Bell. Chicago: University of Chicago Press.

Delaney, Janice, Mary Jane Lupton, and Emily Toth (1988). *The Curse: A Cultural History of Menstruation*. Rev. ed. Urbana: University of Illinois Press.

Douglas, Mary (1966). *Purity and Danger*. London: Routledge & Kegan Paul.

Douglas, Mary (1972). "Deciphering a Meal." *Daedalus* 101: 61–82.

Douglas, Mary (1973). *Natural Symbols: Explorations in Cosmology*. New York: Pantheon.

Douglas, Mary, ed. (1984). *Food in the Social Order: Studies of Food and Festivities in Three American Communities*. New York: Russell Sage Foundation.

Firth, Raymond (1959). *Social Change in Tikopia: Restudy of a Polynesian Community after a Generation*. New York: Macmillan.

Freud, Anna (1946). "The Psychoanalytic Study of Infantile Feeding Disturbances." *The Psychoanalytic Study of the Child: An Annual* 2: 119–32.

Freud, Sigmund (1962). *Three Contributions to the Theory of Sex*. New York: Dutton.

Garfinkel, Paul E., and David M. Garner (1982). *Anorexia Nervosa: A Multidimensional Perspective*. New York: Brunner/Mazel.

Geertz, Clifford (1973). *The Interpretation of Cultures*. New York: Basic Books.

Gilligan, Carol (1981). *In a Different Voice: Psychological Theory and Women's Development*. Cambridge: Harvard University Press.

Goody, Jack (1982). *Cooking, Cuisine and Class: A Study in Comparative Sociology*. New York: Cambridge University Press.

Gordon, Richard A. (1988). "A Sociocultural Interpretation of the Current Epidemic of Eating Disorders." In *The Eating Disorders*, ed. B. J. Blinder, B. F. Chaiting, and R. Goldstein, pp. 151–63. Great Neck, N. Y.: PMA Publishing.

Holmberg, Allan R. (1969). *Nomads of the Long Bow: The Siriono of Eastern Bolivia*. Prospect Heights, Ill.: Waveland.

Kahn, Miriam (1986). *Always Hungry, Never Greedy: Food and the Expression of Gender in a Melanesian Society*. New York: Cambridge University Press.

Katona-Apte, Judit (1975). "Dietary Aspects of Acculturation in South Asia." In *Gastronomy: The Anthropology of Food Habits*, ed. Margaret L. Arnott, pp. 315–26. The Hague: Mouton.

Lawrence, Marilyn (1984). *The Anorexic Experience*. London: Women's Press.

Lee, Richard B. (1979). *The !Kung San: Men, Women and Work in a Foraging Society*. New York: Cambridge University Press.

Lee, Richard B. (1984). *The Dobe !Kung*. New York: Holt, Rinehart & Winston.

Levenkron, Steven (1978). *The Best Little Girl in the World*. New York: Warner.

Levenkron, Steven (1982). *Treating and Overcoming Anorexia Nervosa*. New York: Scribners.

Lévi-Strauss, Claude (1967). *The Elementary Structures of Kinship*. Boston: Beacon.

Lévi-Strauss (1969). *The Raw and the Cooked: Introduction to a Science of Mythology*. Trans. John Weightman and Doreen Weightman. New York: Harper & Row.

Liu, Aimee (1979). *Solitaire*. New York: Harper & Row.

Mackenzie, Margaret (1976). "Self-Control, Moral Responsibility, Competence, and Rationality: Obesity as Failure in American Culture." *Obesity/Bariatric Medecine* 5 (4), 132–33.

Macleod, Sheila (1981). *The Art of Starvation: A Story of Anorexia and Survival*. New York: Schocken.

Malinowski, Bronislaw (1922). *Argonauts of the Western Pacific*. New York: Dutton.

Marshall, Lorna (1976). *The !Kung of Nyae Nyae*. Cambridge: Harvard University Press.

Mauss, Marcel (1967, orig. 1925). *The Gift: Forms and Functions of Exchange in Archaic Societies*. New York: Norton.

Mead, Margaret (1967). *Male and Female*. New York: Morrow.

Meigs, Anna S. (1984). *Food, Sex and Pollution: A New Guinea Religion*. New Brunswick: Rutgers University Press.

Messer, Ellen (1989). "Small but Healthy? Some Cultural Considerations." *Human Organization* 48 (1), forthcoming.

Messina, Maria (1988). "The Odour of Piety." Paper presented at the 87th Annual Meeting of the American Anthropological Association.

Millman, Marcia (1980). *Such a Pretty Face: Being Fat in America*. New York: Norton.

Minuchin, Salvador, Bernice L. Rosman, and Lester Baker (1978). *Psychosomatic Families: Anorexia Nervosa in Context*. Cambridge: Harvard University Press.

Murphy, Yolanda, and Robert F. Murphy (1985). *Women of the Forest*. 2d ed. New York: Columbia University Press.

Nochlin, Linda (1988). *Women, Art, and Power and Other Essays*. New York: Harper & Row.

Orbach, Susie (1978). *Fat Is a Feminist Issue: The Anti-Diet Guide to Permanent Weight Loss*. New York: Paddington.

Orbach, Susie (1982). *Fat is a Feminist Issue II: A Program to Conquer Compulsive Eating*. New York: Berkeley.

Palazzoli, Marie Selvini (1974). *Self-Starvation: From the Intrapsychic to the Transpersonal Approach to Anorexia Nervosa*. London: Chaucer.

Pandian, Jacob (1985). *Anthropology and the Western Tradition: Toward an Authentic Anthropology*. Prospect Heights, Ill : Waveland.

Paul, Lois (1974). "The Mastery of Work and the Mystery of Sex in a Guatemalan Village." In *Women, Culture and Society*, ed. Michelle Zimbalist Rosaldo and Louise Lamphere, pp. 281–99. Stanford: Stanford University Press.

Peacock, James L. (1986). *The Anthropological Lens: Harsh Light, Soft Focus*. New York: Cambridge University Press.

Powdermaker, Hortense (1960). "An Anthropological Approach to the Problem of Obesity." *Bulletin of the New York Academy of Medicine* 36: 286–95.

Quaggiotto, Pamela (1989). Personal communication.

Richards, Audrey I. (1939). *Land, Labour and Diet in Northern Rhodesia: An Economic Study of the Bemba Tribe*. Oxford: Oxford University Press.

Sahlins, Marshall (1972). *Stone Age Economics*. Hawthorne, N. Y.: Aldine.

Schwartz, Hillel (1986). *Never Satisfied: A Cultural History of Diets, Fantasies, and Fat*. New York: Free Press.

Shack, Dorothy (1969). "Nutritional Processes and Personality Development among the Gurage of Ethiopia." *Ethnology* 8 (3), 292–300.

Shack, William (1971). "Hunger, Anxiety and Ritual: Deprivation and Spirit Possession among the Gurage of Ethiopia." *Man* 6 (1), 30–43.

Shostak, Marjorie (1981). *Nisa, the Life and Words of a !Kung Woman*. New York: Vintage.

Siskind, Janet (1973). *To Hunt in the Morning*. New York: Oxford University Press.

Stack, Carol B. (1974). *All Our Kin: Strategies for Survival in a Black Community*. New York: Harper & Row.

Striegel-Moore, Ruth H., Lisa R. Silberstein, and Judith Rodin (1986). "Toward an Understanding of the Risk Factors for Bulimia." *American Psychologist* 41 (3), 246–63.

Styles, Marvalene H. (1980). "Soul, Black Women and Food." In *A Woman's Conflict: The Special Relationship between Women and Food*, ed. Jane Rachel Kaplan, pp. 161–76. Englewood Cliffs, N. J.: Prentice-Hall.

Taggart, James M. (1983). *Nahuat Myth and Social Structure*. Austin: University of Texas Press.

Tambiah, S. J. (1969). "Animals Are Good to Think and Good to Prohibit." *Ethnology* 8 (4), 423–59.

Thomas, Elizabeth Marshall (1959). *The Harmless People*. New York: Knopf.

Turnbull, Colin M. (1972). *The Mountain People*. New York: Simon & Schuster.

Tylor, Sir Edward Burnett (1958, orig. 1871). *Primitive Culture*. New York: Harper & Row.

Verdier, Yvonne (1969). "Pour une ethnologie culinaire." *L'Homme* 9 (1), 49–57.

Weiner, Annette (1988). *The Trobrianders of Papua New Guinea*. New York: Holt, Rinehart & Winston.

Weismantel, M. J. (1988). *Food, Gender and Poverty in the Ecuadorian Andes*. Philadelphia: University of Pennsylvania Press.

Winnick, Myron (1979). *Hunger Disease: Studies by the Jewish Physicians in the Warsaw Ghetto*. New York: Wiley.

Wolf, Eric (1974). *Anthropology*. New York: Norton.

Young, Michael W. (1971). *Fighting with Food: Leadership, Values and Social Control in a Massim Society*. New York: Cambridge University Press.

Young, Michael W. (1986). " 'The Worst Disease': The Cultural Definition of Hunger in Kalauna." In *Shared Wealth and Symbol: Food, Culture and Society in Oceania and Southeast Asia*, ed. Lenore Manderson, pp. 111–26. New York: Cambridge University Press.

WOMEN AS GATEKEEPERS OF FOOD CONSUMPTION: A SOCIOLOGICAL CRITIQUE

Wm. Alex McIntosh and Mary Zey

Social scientists have until very recently neglected the "production of consumption"—that is, the creation of finished goods and services for consumption within the boundaries of the home.[1] Production is usually studied in terms of the economy at large, and the concern of such research tends to be what is produced, how much is produced, and who gets it. Furthermore, analysts view consumption as the *purchase* of goods and services, and are frequently concerned most about distributional differences governed by social class background (cf. Weber 1966; Sobel 1981). When researchers focus on behavior within the household, they shift attention from things to emotions. Karl Marx, for example, recognized the human need for food, clothing, and shelter, but he emphasized their production and distribution; the social circumstances of actual consumption he considered unimportant because they are "outside the economic relation" (Cohen 1978: 103). Talcott Parsons and Robert Bales (1955), on the other hand, differentiated material production, which occurs in the economy, from emotional production, which originates in the family. It is a woman's role to produce a happy, emotionally stable home, but Parsons and Bales ignored the part that physical consumption might play in providing such a home.

The importance of consumption has not been lost on social commentators from colonial times to the present day (Ryan 1983; Beecher 1841;

Beecher and Stowe 1971; Rose 1940). Women have learned the importance of the consumption opportunities they provide in terms of survival
value, moral worth, and self-fulfillment.

Because a good deal of consumption occurs in the home, it has been
assumed to be the province of women. Women are credited with control
over the purchasing, storing, cooking, and serving of food. In addition, they
are perceived as greatly influencing the food habits of family members.

Commentators and scientists from Catharine Beecher (1841) through
Kurt Lewin (1943) to Bernice Martin (1984) have made assumptions
about the domestic sphere that may not survive close scrutiny. Studies of
task distribution and decision making in the family do show that women
make decisions about food purchases and do the actual purchasing, storing, and preparing of food, but observers have drawn the unfounded conclusion that women thus control the flow of food into the family.
Responsibility is not equivalent to *control*. An analogy makes the point
clear: secretaries monitor, direct, classify, and store information, making
them indispensable components of bureaucracy, but others make and
enforce the policies that affect their everyday activities.

The nature and efficacy of "consumption roles" are, because of the fundamental physiological and social consequences, important concerns.
Understanding this role requires that we ascertain the degree to which
women actually control food flow and what additional forces might intervene. In this article we argue that although women have generally been
held responsible for these roles, men, to varying degrees, control their
enactment.[2] We also argue that this ability to control depends on the relative distribution between men and women of certain social resources. The
study of who controls family food thus may tell us much about family
power structure.

We trace the development of the notion that women control the flow of
food into the home and present evidence that questions its truth. Using
exchange theory, we identify sources of power available to husbands and
wives and use them to formulate research hypotheses regarding the degree
of wives' control over family food.

A BRIEF HISTORY OF DOMESTIC POWER

Despite their involvement in production activities both inside and outside
the home, American women have been portrayed from colonial times to
the present in ways that emphasize their domestic responsibilities. Even in
centuries before the Industrial Revolution when women produced food

and income (Ryan 1983; Ulrich 1987), women's status was determined primarily through the performance of domestic roles (Koehler 1980; Folbre 1980). Important among these roles were the acquiring, storing, preserving, and preparing of food for family consumption. Middle-class women saw their production roles contract as a consequence of industrialization and capitalist marketing, thereby increasing their responsibilities for the emotional well-being of family members. Farm and working-class women continued to hold major responsibilities for production and for the generation of income (Osterud 1987; Farnham 1987).

By the mid-19th century, domesticity had been elevated to the level of a religious calling. Magazines and books of the day portrayed domesticity as women's highest aspiration. Thus, one 19th-century writer for a popular magazine effused, "as society is constituted, the true dignity and beauty of female character seem to consist in a right understanding and faithful and cheerful performance of social and family duties" (Farley 1846: 21, quoted in Welter 1978: 320). Others described a woman's position in the home as a "throne."

This ideology, in one guise or another, has reappeared in publications throughout the twentieth century. During the period 1920–1940, for example, women were asked whether they were "100% Mother" and to alter their behavior if they were not (Matthews 1987: 187). And similar advice appeared in the 1950s and 1970s:

> Do you ever think, while in the midst of a pile of dirty dishes, with beds still to make, and children to dress, and ironing staring at you as well as a messy house, "Wasn't I made for better things than this?" And if we listen, the answer seems to echo and re-echo through the house: The routine work we do in our homes every day makes life secure and happy and orderly for those we love the most. The biggest hurdle we have to cross is our approach to our daily tasks. (Johnson 1961: 15)

And: "Of all the persons in the world, none are more important than that crowd we call wives" (Schuller 1974: 9).

Much of this advice literature, as well as more general descriptions of domesticity, included the special part food plays in family life. Women received conflicting counsel regarding meals. Admonishment to provide the healthiest, most thrifty meals was frequent. Women were told that the "health of the nation" depended upon the quality of meals they prepared. Cooking and other aspects of housekeeping were often considered scientific endeavors, successfully undertaken only by those with the proper training and orientation (Matthews 1987; Mintz and Kellogg 1988; Ogden 1986). At the same time, however, the emotional needs and social stability of the family required meals that provided likable food and a pleasant atmosphere. In fact, a wife and mother's success rested as much on the socioemotional aspects of her food provision as on its healthfulness (Gilman 1899; Fredrick 1930, cited in Sachs 1988; Rose 1940; see also Matthaei 1982).

THE GATEKEEPER CONCEPT

In the 1940s Kurt Lewin (1943) developed a term that has become an integral concept in the field of nutrition: the "gatekeeper." Arising out of an experimental program designed to change the shopping habits of women, the concept of gatekeeper reflects the perception that women control the flow of goods, specifically food, into the household. Lewin (p. 37) argued that we can discover why people eat what they eat if we learn how food comes to the table. Food gets to the table through what he calls "channels" such as the grocery store, the garden, and the refrigerator. The selection of channels and the foods that travel through them is under the control of the gatekeeper. In his study of 107 midwestern housewives Lewin found that these women control "all of the channels except gardening, and even there the husband(s) seldom control this channel alone. Children are never mentioned as controlling any of the channels, although they undoubtedly influence the decisions indirectly through their rejection of food put before them" (p. 40).

For the forty-five years since Lewin's work, many dietetics and nutrition textbooks have referred, in discussions of children's and adolescents' dietary habits, to the gatekeeper role played by women (Whitney and Cataldo 1983; Bass et al. 1979; Gifft et al. 1972). The concept has also been adopted by the relatively new field of nutritional anthropology (Freedman 1977).

The social sciences have continued to view the family as the institutional setting for the meeting of many of the most important needs of human beings. In particular, families provide the mechanisms for reproduction, status placement, and socialization (Adams 1975). The family is expected by its members to meet their needs for affection, companionship, openness, and material sustenance. The family also provides the setting for most consumption and leisure activities (Allan 1985). Finally, some writers have claimed that families provide a major service to the capitalist system by "reproducing labor," that is, by preparing adult members for the day-to-day tasks of employment and children for future work roles (Berch 1982: 93). Christopher Lasch (1977) has described the family as a last "haven" in an otherwise "heartless" world, an ideal similar to that suggested in the

19th century. Such commentaries continue to stress that women are ultimately responsible for creating the environment necessary to meet needs,
provide consumption and leisure opportunities, and reproduce labor.

Thus does the work by Lewin and by social scientists writing since his
pioneering work serve further to legitimate the idea of women's essential
domesticity.

The picture we have constructed suggests the importance of women's
domestic roles and the centrality of meals to them. None of what we have
said thus far necessarily raises doubts about who controls the flow of food.
But several other elements are associated with domesticity and the relationship between husbands and wives; once included, they do raise questions about ultimate control over what the family eats. These elements
include the views that women are intellectually inferior and that women's
roles, though important, are less so than men's, thereby justifying men's
continued control over economic resources.

THE GATEKEEPER IN CONTEXT

During the colonial period, women were frequently described as irrespon-
sible and incapable of practical decisions, and although this image
changed during the 19th century, the view of women as intellectually inferior survived (Harris 1978: 40). Toward the end of the 19th century,
Darwinian and Lamarkian thinkers went so far as to describe the home and
homemaking as evolutionary backwaters that impeded societal advance-
ment (Matthews 1987).

From the beginning of this century, women have been admonished to be
scientific and efficient. But any elevation of women's status that such pre-
scriptions might have achieved was undercut by the appearance of new
household products: food sold in ready-to-eat form and appliances that
reduced the drudgery of housework. Increasingly, writers portrayed
domesticity as both easy and frivolous (Margolis 1984: 149), and popular
publications described women as lazy, immature, impractical, and selfish.
Because domesticity apparently demanded no more than sharp shopping
skills, many argued that women were no longer pulling their weight
(Matthews 1987). Many recent advice books deal with the apparent contradiction of housework's being viewed as both "scientific" and "unimportant" by suggesting that housework is important but less important than
what men do (Morgan 1973). This advice mimics what women heard
during the 19th century (Welter 1978).

In the relationship between husband and wife, it is no surprise to find that women have been, to varying degrees, *expected* to be deferential if not submissive to men, particularly their husbands. Social sanctions of various sorts, from corporal punishment during the colonial period (Koehler 1980) to social ostracism more recently, have helped enforce this form of inequality (Matthews 1987).

Even when women were admired for their moral superiority, they were advised to yield gracefully when their husbands resisted their entreaties (Welter 1978). For example, some commentators argued that women make the food choices but recognized that husbands could either "simplify or complicate the problem considerably" (Wood et al. 1932: 206).

Finally, despite women's responsibility for the everyday tasks of housework, men have generally controlled the family finances, particularly in middle-class households (e.g., Spruill 1982).[3] In part this control reflects vestiges of patriarchy (Folbre 1980), but it has received ideological support from notions of women as overly emotional and thus irrational.

Current views of women suggest that at least middle-class men are becoming more likely to credit women with practicality on a par with their own. Nevertheless, recent studies show that men continue to control the pursestrings in many families, with consequences for women's everyday household activities and decisions (Wilson 1987; Haygood 1939). This research also finds that men continue to make the major family financial decisions and intrude on the "minor" ones (Blumstein and Schwartz 1983: 151; Hunt 1978).[4]

These elements of women's domestic roles in relation to food suggest that women are in charge of purchasing and storing food and preparing meals but that men's control over the family finances, women's obligations to produce a harmonious family life, and women's deference toward men all increase the likelihood that men will ultimately control family food decisions. The small amount of contemporary research to touch on the issue of food control reinforces the impression that women maintain little power over their own consumption-producing activities.

CONTEMPORARY RESEARCH ON THE GATEKEEPER ROLE

Present research casts doubt on the inherent power of the domestic role played by women, but it also suggests that women continue to be the chief decision makers regarding food selection for the family (Centers et al. 1971; Davis and Rigraux 1974; Allan 1985). Other researchers, however, suggest that concern for serving food that will please family members is paramount in this decision making (Sutor and Barbour 1975). A Missouri study finds that the general food preferences of fathers took precedence over those of mothers (Burt and Hertzler 1978). Research by Robert Schafer and Joe Bohlen (1977) shows that when husbands object to the serving of a new dish, 68 percent of wives report they would not serve the dish again. More specifically, Lewin (1943) finds that housewives regard meat as a special food for their husbands, suggesting that at least for this item the desires of the husband are important. Similarly, Zey-Ferrell and McIntosh (1987) found that Texas women's intent to consume less beef in the future is affected much more strongly by their husbands' views *and* the women's wish to comply with those views than by their own views regarding the healthfulness, safety, social desirability, or cost of beef.

The most challenging objection to the gatekeeper thesis comes from several studies of lower-class households in England which show that when a meal is not to the husband's liking, he may react with extreme violence (Murcott 1983; Ellis 1983). Another English study finds that when divorced women recall conflicts that lead to the dissolution of the marriage, they frequently cite arguments over what meals were served (Burgoyne and Clarke 1983). We lack comparable studies of American families, but these English results suggest that conflicts in lower-class households may, on occasion, revolve around food.

There is a seeming disjunction between the expectation that women control food decisions and the limited reality of such control. A discussion of power is in order. This concept not only explains why women have less control over food decisions than has been suggested, it also lays the groundwork for fuller investigation of this issue.

POWER, INFLUENCE, CONTROL: SOME HYPOTHESES

The concepts of power, influence, and control are essential to our understanding of the concept of women's domestic role, especially its food-related responsibilities and its relationship to the exercise of power in the home. To determine who controls the flow of food into the household, we must examine the nature of family power, differentiate among its sources, and distinguish it from influence and control.

Maximiliane Szinovacz (1987: 652) defines *power* as the "net ability or capability of action to produce or cause intended outcomes or effects, particularly on the behavior of others, or on others' outcomes." Power gives people the capacity to make things happen, including the capacity to make others see to it that those things happen. It is generally assumed that this capacity is held differentially.

One form of power, *authority*, derives from legitimate rights to get certain others to do one's bidding. Authority is almost always backed up by legal and economic resources; husband-fathers, given our current legal and economic expectations, generally possess the greater share of authority in families. In some states, men can still dispose of "family" property, such as land, without having to consult their wives (Elbert 1987: 259). *Coercion* reflects a differential in brute strength; one person can force others to do things because of the threat of physical force. The degree to which coercion and legitimate power overlap varies by society. In the United States, for example, the police may legitimately use physical force under certain circumstances. Spouses may not; but the legal system (which has certain legitimate concerns about what occurs within families) has frequently looked the other way when husbands have used coercion to control financial and sexual resources.

Those with little power may try to use *influence*, which is informal and rests in a person's ability to persuade, manipulate, convince, or in some indirect way shape the decisions of others. Influence is a form of power to the extent that others end up doing what otherwise they would not have done. Finally, *control* encompasses all types of power but also has implications for supervising, monitoring, and in some cases executing the tasks to implement a decision.

Some argue that women have accepted the idea of "separate spheres" and the power differential it implies simply because of socialization. Women accept a lesser status because they are taught from an early age to do so (Frieze 1978), and social sanctions complete whatever socialization misses. Such sanctions are generally at the level of gossip, but failure by women to adhere to some norms (such as those governing child care, for instance) can result in intervention by the legal system.

Contemporary theorists argue, however, that issues of domestic power are largely resource-based and that culture both reflects and supports resource differentials between men and women (cf. Allan 1985; Curtis 1986). Nevertheless, some of these observers suggest that through labor force participation, status production, control over household technology, and emotional or sexual manipulation, women do possess power. This suggestion implies that women possess potentially powerfull resources. We turn to a discussion of these resources and their hypothesized effects on food control.

RESOURCES AND POWER

Social exchange theory views social interaction as an exchange of resources. Individuals give up resources under their control in order to obtain the resources they lack from others who possess them. At times individuals exchange compliance with others' wishes for access to what they need.

Thus resources, particularly economic resources, provide power. Anthropologists have noted that in those societies where women produce goods considered to have economic value, women's power is greater than in societies where what they produce is not considered economically valuable (Friedl 1975; Shlegel 1977; Stichter 1988; Leacock 1981; see also Todd 1987). This observation, as we shall see, is vitally important for understanding power and control in contemporary American families. Hygienic homes, nutritious meals, and the satisfaction of emotional and social needs have, by current standards, low economic value. If wives did not produce these things, however, husbands would have to do so themselves, pay others to produce them, or do without.

In the United States, particularly today, the major source of the father-husband's ability to control the behavior of wives and children is the income he brings home. Numerous studies show that a husband's power increases in direct proportion to his earnings (cf. Blumstein and Schwartz 1983). So important is this resource for men that when they lose their jobs, their power over both their wives and children diminishes considerably (Komorovsky 1962).

Education, prestige, and age are also considered sources of power, but less important ones than economic resources. Some men, particularly those of lower-class origin, rely upon force to continue their exercise of power. In addition, the literature on family power has demonstrated that net rather than gross resource control is the key to determining who has power. Family members in need of resources become dependent on those who possess more of those resources. As money is frequently the key to other resources, family members become most dependent on the member with the highest income.

Labor Force Participation

Most studies of the effects of women's participation in the labor force have devoted much attention to the modern-day equivalent of the notion of "separate spheres": the division of household labor (cf. England and Farkas 1986; Berk 1985; Pleck 1985; Waite 1978; Bianchi and Spain 1986;

Fox and Nichols 1983; Model 1981; Nichols and Metzen 1982). These researchers suggest that home and work outside the home remain separate in that women continue to be largely responsible for household consumption. Of interest, however, is the finding that a small percentage of men have taken over responsibilities for the preparation of specific meals and grocery shopping (Berk and Berk 1979: 229–234).

Studies that examine control as well as division of labor indicate, as predicted, that women who work do increase their control over major family decisions and that power is thus more likely to be shared. The amount of power sharing, however, depends on the wife's income relative to her husband's (Blood and Wolfe 1960). As hers approaches his in magnitude, power sharing increases. However, none of these studies deals directly with food decisions. Unfortunately, Schafer and Bohlen (1977) do not take into account the work status of the wife and so cannot assess the effects of relative salaries on decisions related to food.

When married women participate in the labor force, they create opportunities for gains as well as losses of control over the food that flows into the household. Women who work are less able to supervise at home and so may actually lose some control over what their children eat. Some women reclaim control through outside sources of help. Other family members, neighbors, or hired help (e.g., sitters, daycare centers) may provide substitute supervision. The complexity of the issues suggests somewhat contradictory hypotheses. Women who work outside the household but whose income and prestige do not approach those of their husbands have less control over food, we posit, than women who do not work outside the household. This hypothesis holds for all socioeconomic groups and probably for most ethnic groups as well. In addition, women who work outside the household but whose income and prestige are equal to or exceed those of their husbands have greater control over food than women who do not work and women who work but have lower status than their husbands do. This control may *increase* when women employ outside sources of help. We infer from the literature that this hypothesis will not hold for women of lower socioeconomic status or non-Anglo ethnicity.

Status Production

A women might acquire a greater say over food decisions by making the results of housework, particularly with regard to food, more valuable to her husband. Upper-middle- and upper-class women do so through the production of status for their husbands: through the maintenance of pleasant surroundings, the purchase of "objects of art and other valued goods—all items that are visible to a community of peers" (Coser 1987: 2). Status production work consists of activities such as entertainment that support the husband's career, community work such as membership in voluntary organizations, and management of children's careers (piano, tennis, and other lessons) (Kanter 1977). Rose Laub Coser (1987) argues that such activities lead husbands to relinquish some power.

For the majority of women, however, status production is irrelevant; most husbands do not bring their homes into their careers. On the other hand, those husbands who do need the help of their wives may come to trust their wives' judgment because of positive assessments from coworkers and supervisors who have had the opportunity to consume "produced status." Though fully aware of the measurement problems implied by abstractions such as "status production," we hypothesize that the greater the status production by wives, the greater will be their *control* over the flow of food into the family.

Household Technology

Organizational studies have long speculated about the effects of technology on organizational power (Scott 1987). Attention has frequently focused on increased control over other persons brought about by control over technology. Household technology has developed in recent decades and is generally controlled by the homemaker. Has the homemaker's power increased as a consequence? We think it has not.

Technology is linked to organizational structure and thus has implications for power (Woodward 1958; Hage and Aiken 1979). For instance, technology that routinizes production leads to a more formal, structured, bureaucratic organization, and in particular, authority is more centralized in such settings. On the other hand, where technology is associated with craft production, organizations are less formal and less centralized. Some household tasks are routine: making beds, washing dishes, shopping. Meal preparation is more like craftwork.

Peter Blau and his associates (1979) note that technology which routinizes work lessens the skills required to perform the work. Technology requiring advanced skills is frequently associated with nonroutine tasks, such as computer programming, and thus leads to decentralization of decision making and greater autonomy for the workforce.

We suggest that household technology has little effect on the power structure of the household. As David Hickson and associates (1979) note, technology affects the distribution of power among persons directly involved in the use of that technology; the "wider administrative and hierarchical structure" is unaffected (p. 105). For women who already have sole responsibility for household work, technology that routinizes that work, such as washing machines or dishwashers, is not likely either to enhance or to reduce their power in the family. Technology that emphasizes craftsmanship, such as food processors, has no bearing on the distribution of power between husband and wife if the husband is not directly involved in these household tasks. The wife's power is affected only if technology allows her to spend time on work outside the home, thus increasing her salary and reducing the salary differential between her and her spouse.

Ruth Schwartz Cowan (1983: 209) argues that dishwashers and microwaves make it possible to "still manage to get a decent dinner on the table that night and clean clothes on everyone's back the next morning." Less generous assessments suggest that more equipment increases rather than lightens women's household burdens (Robinson 1980). Washing machines, vacuum cleaners, and dish washers, for instance, usually increase by 4–5 minutes per activity per day the time spent doing housework. S. Manning (1968), focusing entirely on equipment for producing meals, found that the greater the number of cooking appliances and other equipment the more time women spent producing meals. The only form of technology to reduce time spent was the microwave. Bettina Berch (1982: 120) describes the equipment-time anomaly as "managing consumption."

However household technology may affect housework efficiency, we argue that it has little impact on the issue of control. We hypothesize that no relationship will be observed between the amount or nature of household technology and women's control over food.

Sex and Love

Researchers have tended to ignore sex as a family-power resource, but it appears that women and, perhaps to a lesser extent, men use sexual favors to extract compliance from their spouses. Research on lower-class families lends weight to this assertion (Komarovsky 1962; Rubin 1976). Marilyn Luxton (1980) finds that working-class women deliberately engage in sexual manipulation to obtain expensive household appliances. We know less about the use of sex as a bargaining chip in middle- and upper-class families. We know, however, that literature directed at women has long advised them, explicitly or implicitly, to withhold sexual favors in order to obtain compliance (Harris 1971; Morgan 1973; Schlafly 1977).

Related to sexual resources are emotional resources. Once again, researchers have tended to overlook or discount emotional attachment as a source of power, but some have found evidence of its importance

(Safilios-Rothschild 1976). Because "love" is difficult to quantify, researchers assume either that two people involved in a relationship love each other equally or that love is not really a resource. Some have argued, however, that within a couple the person less emotionally attached has power over the other. Although we might anticipate that women receive greater emotional benefits in a marriage, research shows the opposite: the majority of married men report greater emotional rewards from marriage than do married women. It is again unclear, however, whether women use this potential resource to extract compliance from men, and if they do, whether its use varies by social class and ethnicity. Research by Lee Rainwater and others (1962) shows that working-class women report high levels of emotional dependence on their husbands but doubt their ability to maintain their husband's love. Yet John Scanzoni (1982) reports in his studies of couples that as men's socioeconomic status increases, so does their satisfaction with the companionship, empathy, and emotional love provided by their wives. And Schafer and Bohlen (1971) find that husbands are most likely to say they would use referent power to persuade their wives not to serve a new dish again. The referent power of the husband relies on his ability to persuade her that he is a significant other with whom she should wish to comply. Forty-seven percent of male respondents selected this form of power. Interestingly, 43 percent of wives (a plurality) recognized this was the form of power their husbands would use. Furthermore, 76 percent of wives reported they would yield under such circumstances and not serve the dish again.

Two hypotheses are suggested. First, if the wife has the greater emotional stake in the marriage, she will exercise less control over the flow of food into the house. Second, when women have the smaller emotional stake, they will be more likely to withhold sex and other expressions of love and will have more control over the flow of food. These hypotheses, however, may not hold strictly for all segments of the class structure or all ethnic groups.

CONCLUSIONS

We began with the premise that consumption is sufficiently important to warrant the same attention production has received. Students of women's roles have relied too long on untested assumptions about women and women's work to address questions about who controls what we have called "the production of consumption." The literature on women's roles tends to be polemical, or theoretical, or empirical—rarely are the theoretical and the empirical joined in single work. Thus some writers describe women's roles from Marxist or from Parsonian perspectives, but their empirical counterparts make little attempt to relate their findings to theory of any sort. Other segments of this literature *do* join theory and data by applying inferences from exchange theory to women's roles. Marriage (and, to a degree, family life) is viewed as a series of exchanges among role-incumbents whose power and responsibilities are largely determined by the resources (economic, emotional, sexual, muscular) they can bring to bear. Commentators have criticized this approach for its lack of attention to everyday decisions, and indeed, it has focused on general husband-father versus wife-mother issues as opposed to the actual issue of control of food.

This body of research also suffers from methodological shortcomings. A good deal of the research relies upon self-reported descriptions of power over general decisions, only a few of which deal with food issues. Some concern has been expressed that self-reports generate "socially desirable" responses from interviewees: for example, male respondents may not own up to doing laundry, a task generally identified as "female." In addition, men and women may be unwilling to report the use of either coercion or sex to achieve desired behavior from spouses. Such methodological short-comings call for approaches that go beyond the usual fixed-question, fixed-response survey.

Studies that follow Lillian Breslow Rubin (1976) and Scanzoni (1970) may help unveil patterns of daily food decisions and actions and who ulti-mately controls them. Rubin uses general open-ended questions that allow her to pursue topics as they arise during face-to-face interviews with mari-tal partners. Scanzoni uses fixed questions but open-ended responses. For instance, he asks respondents to list "the four things that you and your [spouse] have disagreed about most often." After the listing of these four areas of disagreement comes the query "When you disagree about———— [the first thing cited] who usually gets his[5] way, you or your [spouse]?" for each of the four things listed.

New studies undertaken to explore these important issues must take into account differences in race and ethnicity, region, and social class. The available literature suggests a woman's control over food may be smaller if she is a Hispanic, a white Southerner, or poorly paid relative to her hus-band. Stage in the lifecycle may also make a difference, in that conflict and disagreement increase after marriage but decrease to lower levels once adults reach middle age (generally coinciding with the departure from home of the last child).

Finally, research on issues of food control subsumes the problems encountered in all studies of everyday life. Survey research works well when one asks about behavior that is either nonroutine or, if routine, of some symbolic or self-defining importance. Vacationing in a new place, going to church, or attending weight-loss meetings either mark a departure from everyday events or reflect values or aspects of self-esteem; they are more likely to be recalled than trips to the store, what was served for dinner a week ago Thursday, or what was purchased at the grocery store last shopping day. Dietary methodologists illustrate the problem: generally they find that memories of what was eaten more than a day ago are problematic, and even determining what was eaten over the past 24 hours requires a good deal of probing by skilled interviewers (Evers and McIntosh 1977; Sanjur 1982).

Researchers have successfully used surveys to collect information about food beliefs, attitudes, and behavioral changes of a nonroutine sort; one example is cutting back on the amount of red meat eaten because of stories in the mass media or advice from physicians. In our own research we have found that survey respondents have little trouble answering questions about their perceptions and knowledge of beef. When asked how often they read about or discuss specific items of food, food in general, or food in relation to health, most respondents answer "infrequently to never." Everyday experience, however, suggests that people often discuss what they are eating, often in the very act of doing so. Likewise, family members frequently discuss weight problems, whether too much salt is unhealthy, and the price of food. The disjuncture between what people say they do and what they actually do seems, in this case, to be due largely to the subject's routine nature and lack of major symbolic importance.

In-depth studies of small numbers of families should be the starting point. In the process of observing and probing, researchers often uncover code words and symbols, knowledge of which should allow us to ask more informed questions about routine, mundane aspects of food beliefs and behavior. In addition, observations of everyday activities and discussions should serve to stimulate questions about how food items came to be purchased and prepared. The hypotheses we have provided can elucidate the context in which actual decision-making takes place and the role resources play. In addition, such studies will help determine the degree to which actual behavior deviates from decisions: To what degree do situational factors intervene to force a change in meal timing, meal preparation, and food choices? Answers to such questions may result in the modification of our hypotheses. But only when we have a clearer idea of questions to ask and how to ask them can we proceed to test the hypotheses suggested in this article.

NOTES

An earlier version of this article was presented at the Annual Meeting of the Association for the Study of Food and Society, Aquinas College, Grand Rapids, Michigan, in April 1987.

Thanks are extended to Melonie Hopkins and Cecilia Garza for their help in locating and deciphering data sources. Also, Letitia Alston and Sara Alpern made useful suggestions, tempering our sometimes zealous interpretations of both sociological theory and history. Finally, the reviewers provided a major redirection, rendering the article far more interesting in its final form.

1. Neglect by historians stems, in part, from a lack of materials that describe the everyday dynamics of decision making before the 1950s.
2. We wish to make it clear that when we discuss men's ultimate control of food, we are making empirical rather than normative assertions. Also, control over food and surrounding issues likely varies by race, ethnicity, religion, and even sexual preference. To create a more nearly universal model of food control would have required more space than a journal can permit and access to a great deal of additional materials. Although we make occasional statements about other groups in both text and footnotes, this article pertains primarily to white Anglo-Americans.
3. Adult females in immigrant, working-class, and black families (both before and after slavery ended) frequently made major family decisions and controlled the family budget (Aschenbrenner 1975; Degler 1980; Stack 1974).
4. One study of lower-class Mexican-American families indicates that in more than 50 percent of these families, men participate in decisions concerning how much to spend on food and what foods to buy (Yetley et al. 1978), apparently as the husband accompanies his wife in grocery shopping. Williams (1988), though not specifically studying food decisions, does indicate that many Mexican-American women of both working- and middle-class backgrounds have expanded their roles and the power to act that goes with them. It is unclear, however, whether this increase in control extends to food.
5. The use of the pronoun "his" implies to the respondent that the response should be "the husband." This question may predispose the respondent. We suggest gender-neutral terminology in future research.

REFERENCES

Adams, Bert M. 1975. *The Family: A Sociological Interpretation.* 2d ed. Chicago: Rand McNally.

Allan, Graham. 1985. *Family Life: Domestic Roles and Social Organization.* New York: Basil Blackwell.

Aschenbrenner, Joyce. 1975. *Life-lines: Black Families in Chicago.* New York: Holt, Rinehart & Winston.

Bass, Mary Ann, Lucille Wakefield, and Kathryn Kolasa. 1979. *Community Nutrition and Individual Behavior.* Minneapolis, Minn.: Burgess.

Beecher, Catharine E. 1841. *A Treatise on Domestic Economy for the Use of Young Ladies at Home and at School.* Boston: Marsh, Capen, Lyon & Webb.

Beecher, Catharine E., and Harriet Beecher Stowe. 1971. *The American Woman's Home.* New York: Arno and the New York Times.

Berch, Bettina. 1982. *The Endless Day: The Political Economy of Women and Work.* San Diego, Calif.: Harcourt Brace Jovanovich.

Berk, Richard A., and Sarah Fenstermaker Berk. 1979. *Labor and Leisure at Home: Content and Organization of the Household Day.* Beverly Hills, Calif.: Sage.

Berk, Sarah Fenstermaker. 1985. *The Gender Factor: The Allocation of Work in American Households.* New York: Plenum Press.

Bianchi, Suzanne M., and Daphne Spain. 1986. *American Women in Transition*. New York: Russell Sage Foundation.

Blau, Peter M., Cecilia McHugh Falke, William McKinley, and Phelps Tracey. 1979. "Technology and Organization in Manufacturing." In Mary Zey-Ferrell, ed. *Readings on Dimensions of Organizations*, pp. 129–150. Santa Monica, Calif.: Goodyear.

Blood, Robert O., Jr., and Donald M. Wolfe. 1960. *Husbands and Wives*. New York: Free Press.

Blumstein, Philip, and Pepper Schwartz. 1983. *American Couples: Money, Work, and Sex*. New York: William Morrow.

Burgoyne, Jacqueline, and David Clarke. 1983. "You Are What You Eat: Food and Family Reconstitution." In Ann Murcott, ed. *The Sociology of Food and Eating: Essays on the Sociological Significance of Food*, pp. 152–163. Aldershot, England: Gower.

Burt, J. V., and A. V. Hertzler. 1978. "Parental Influence on Child's Food Preference." *Journal of Nutrition Education* 10: 123–134.

Centers, Richard, Bertram R. Haven, and Aroldo Rodrigues. 1971. "Conjugal Power Structure: A Re-examination." *American Sociological Review* 36: 264–278.

Cohen, G. A. 1978. *Karl Marx's Theory of History: A Defense*. Princeton: Princeton University Press.

Coser, Rose Laub. 1987. "Power Lost and Status Gained: A Step in the Direction of Sex Equality." In Kai Erikson, ed. *On Work and Alienation*, forthcoming. New Haven: Yale University Press.

Cott, Nancy F. 1977. *The Bonds of Womanhood: "Women's Sphere" in New England, 1780–1835*. New Haven: Yale University Press.

Cowan, Ruth Schwartz. 1983. *More Work for Mother: The Ironies of Household Technology from the Open Hearth to the Microwave*. New York: Basic Books.

Curtis, Richard F. 1986. "Household and Family in Theory on Inequality." *American Sociological Review* 51: 168–183.

David, Harry L., and Benny P. Rigraux. 1974. "Perception of Marital Roles in Decision Processes." *Journal of Consumer Research* 1: 51–62.

Degler, Carl N. 1980. *At Odds: Woman and the Family in America from the Revolution to the Present*. New York: Oxford University Press.

Elbert, Sarah, 1987. "Amber Waves of Grain: Women's Work in New York Farm Families." In Carol Groneman and Mary Beth Norton, eds. *"To Toil the Livelong Day": America's Women at Work, 1780–1980*, pp. 250–268. Ithaca: Cornell University Press.

Ellis, Rhian. 1983. "The Way to a Man's Heart: Food in the Violent Home." In Ann Murcott, ed. *The Sociology of Food and Eating: Essays on the Sociological Significance of Food*, pp. 164–171. Aldershot, England: Gower.

England, Paula, and George Farkas. 1986. *Households, Employment and Gender*. New York: Aldine.

Evers, Susan, and Wm. Alex McIntosh. 1977. "Social Indicators of Human Nutrition." *Social Indicators Research* 4: 185–205.

Farnham, Christie. 1987. "Sapphire? The Issue of Dominance in the Slave Family, 1830–1865." In Carol Groneman and Mary Beth Norton, eds. *"To Toil the Livelong Day": America's Women at Work, 1780–1980*, pp. 68–83. Ithaca: Cornell University Press.

Folbre, Nancy. 1980. "Patriarchy in Colonial New England." *Review of Radical Economics* 12: 4–13.

Fox, Karen D., and Sharon V. Nichols. 1983. "The Time Crunch: Wife's Employment and Family Work." *Journal of Family Issues* 4: 61–82.

Freedman, Robert L. 1977. "Nurtritional Anthropology." In Thomas K. Fitzgerald, ed. *Nutrition and Anthropology in Action*, pp. 1–23. Assen: Van Gorcum.

Friedl, Ernestine. 1975. *Women and Men: An Anthropologist's View*. New York: Holt, Rinehart & Winston.

Frieze, Irene H. 1978. *Women and Sex Roles*. New York: W. W. Nortan.

Gifft, Helen H., Marjorie B. Washborn, and Gail G. Harrison. 1972. *Nutrition, Behavior, and Change.* Englewood Cliffs, N.J.: Prentice-Hall.

Gilman, Charlotte P. S. 1899. *Women and Economics: A Study of the Economic Relations between Men and Women as a Factor in Social Evaluation.* Boston: Small, Maynard.

Hage, Jerald, and Michael Aiken. 1979. "Routine Technology, Social Structure, and Organizational Goals." In Mary Zey-Ferrell, ed. *Readings on Dimension of Organizations*, pp. 150–164. Santa Monica, Calif.: Goodyear.

Harris, Barbara J. 1978. *Beyond Her Sphere: Women and the Professions in American History.* Westport, Conn.: Greenwood Press.

Haygood, Margret Jarman. 1939. *Mothers of the South: Portraiture of the White Tenant Farm Woman.* Chapel Hill: University of North Carolina.

Hickson, David J., D. S. Pugh, and Diana C. Plesey. 1979. "Operations Technology and Organization Structure: An Empirical Reappraisal." In Mary Zey-Ferrell, ed. *Readings on Dimensions of Organizations*, pp. 86–109. Santa Monica, Calif.: Goodyear.

Hunt, P. 1978. "Cash Transactions and Household Tasks." *Sociological Review* 26: 555–571.

Johnson, Charlene. 1961. "Do You Ever Think...?" *Beautiful Homemaking*, no. 110, pp. 14–19.

Kanter, Rosabeth Moss. 1977. *Men and Women of the Corporation.* New York: Basic Books.

Koehler, Lyle. 1980. *A Search for Power: The "Weaker Sex" in Seventeenth-Century New England.* Urbana: University of Illinois Press.

Komorovsky, Mirra. 1940. *The Unemployed Man and His Family.* New York: Dryden Press.

Komorovsky, Mirra. 1962. *Blue Collar Marriage.* New York: Vintage Books.

Lasch, Christopher. 1977. *Haven in a Heartless World: The Family Besieged.* New York: Basic Books.

Leacock, Eleanor Burke. 1981. *Myths of Male Dominance: Collected Articles on Women Cross-culturally.* New York: Monthly Review Press.

Lewin, Kurt. 1943. "Forces behind Food Habits and Methods of Change." In *The Problem of Changing Food Habits*, pp. 35–65. Bulletin no. 108. Washington, D.C.: National Academy of Science, National Research Council.

Luxton, Marilyn. 1980. *More than a Labor of Love.* Toronto: Women's Educational Press.

Manning, S. 1968. "Time in Household Tasks by Indiana Families." *Purdue University Research Bulletin*, no. 837.

Margolis, Maxine L. 1984. *Mothers and Such: Views of American Women and Why They Changed.* Berkeley: University of California Press.

Martin, Bernice. 1984. "'Mother Wouldn't Like It!' Housework as Magic." *Theory, Culture, and Society* 2: 19–36.

Matthaei, Julie A. 1982. *An Economic History of Women in America: Women's Work, the Sexual Division of Labor, and the Development of Capitalism.* New York: Schocken Books.

Matthews, Glenna. 1987. *Just a Housewife: The Rise and Fall of Domesticity in the United States.* New York: Oxford University Press.

Mintz, Steven, and Susan Kellogg. 1988. *Domestic Revolutions: A Social History of American Family Life.* New York: Free Press.

Model, Suzanne. 1981. "Housework by Husbands: Determinants and Implications." *Journal of Family Issues* 2: 225–237.

Morgan, Marabel. 1973. *The Total Woman.* Old Tappan, N.Y.: Fleming H. Revell.

Murcott, Ann. 1983. "It's is a Pleasure to Cook for Him ... : Food, Mealtimes and Gender in Some South Wales Households." In E. Garmarnikov, ed. *The Public and the Private*, pp. 97–107. London: Heinemann.

Nichols, Sharon Y., and Edward Metzen. 1982. "Impact of Wife's Employment upon Husband's Housework." *Journal of Family Issues* 3: 199–216.

Ogden, Annegret S. 1986. *The Great American Housewife: From Helpmate to Wage Earner, 1776–1986.* Westport, Conn.: Greenwood Press.

Osterud, Nancy Grey. 1987. "'She Helped Me Hay It as Good as a Man': Relations among Women and Men in an Agricultural Community." In Carol Groneman and Mary Beth

Norton, eds. *"To Toil the Livelong Day": America's Women at Work, 1780–1980*, pp. 87–97. Ithaca: Cornell University Press.

Persons, Talcott, and Robert F. Bales. 1955. *Family, Socialization, and Interaction Process*. Glencoe, Ill.: Free Press.

Pleck, Joseph. 1985. *Working Wives, Working Husbands*. Beverly Hills, Calif.: Sage.

Preteceille, Edmond. 1977. "Social Needs and State Monopoly Capitalism." In Preteceille and Jean-Pierre Terrail, eds. *Capitalism, Consumption and Needs*, pp. 82–149. Oxford: Basil Blackwell.

Rainwater, Lee, Richard P. Coleman, and Gerald Handel. 1962. *Working Man's Wife*. New York: Macfadden Books.

Robinson, John P. 1980. "Housework Technology and Household Work." In Sarah Fenstermaker Berk, ed. *Women and Household Labor*, pp. 53–68. Beverly Hills, Calif.: Sage.

Rose, Mary Swartz. 1940. *Feeding the Family*. New York: Macmillan.

Rubin, Lillian Breslow. 1976. *Worlds of Pain: Life in the Working-Class Family*. New York: Basic Books.

Ryan, Mary P. 1983. *Womanhood in America: From Colonial Times to the Present*. 3d ed. New York: Franklin Watts.

Sachs, Carolyn. 1988. "The Commodification of the U.S. Food System: Historical Shifts in Women's Work." Presented at the Annual Meeting of the Rural Sociological Society, Athens, Georgia.

Safilios-Rothschild, Constantina. 1976. *Contemporary Marriage: Structure, Dynamics, and Therapy*. Boston: Little, Brown.

Safilios-Rothschild, Constantina. 1969. "Patterns of Familial Power and Influence." *Sociological Focus* 2: 71.

Sanjur, Diva. 1982. *Social and Cultural Perspectives in Nutrition*. Englewood Cliffs, N.J.: Prentice-Hall.

Scanzoni, John. 1982. *Sexual Bargaining: Power Politics in the American Marriage*. 2d ed. Chicago: University of Chicago Press.

Schafer, Robert, and Joe M. Bohlen. 1977. "The Exchange of Conjugal Power and Its Effects on Family Food Consumption." *Home Economics Research Journal* 5: 124–134.

Schlafly, Phyllis. 1977. *The Power of the Positive Woman*. New York: Arlington House.

Schlegel, Alice. 1977. "An Overview." In Schlegel, ed. *Sexual Stratification: A Cross-Cultural View*, pp. 344–357. New York: Columbia University Press.

Schuller, Robert H. 1974. "What Does a Man Really Want in a Wife?" In *Power Ideas for a Happy Home*, pp. 7–10. Old Tappan, N.Y.: Fleming H. Revell.

Scott, W. Richard. 1987. *Organizations: Rational, Natural, and Open Systems*. Englewood Cliffs, N.J.: Prentice-Hall.

Sobel, Michael E. 1981. *Lifestyle and Social Structure: Concepts, Definitions, and Analyses*. New York: Academic Press.

Spruill, Julia Cherry. 1982. "Housewives and Their Helpers." In Lindak Kerber and Jane De Hart Mathews, eds. *Women's America: Refocusing on the Past*, pp. 223–235. New York: Oxford University Press.

Stack, Carol B. 1974. *All Our Kin: Strategies for Survival in a Black Community*. New York: Harper & Row.

Stichter, Sharon B. 1988. "The Middle-class Family in Kenya: Changes in Gender Relations." In Stichter and Jane L. Parpart, eds. *Patriarchy and Class: African Women in the Home and in the Workforce*, pp. 177–204. Boulder, Colo.: Westview Press.

Sutor, Carol B., and Helen F. Barbour. 1975. "Identifying Food Related Values of Low-Income Mothers." *Home Economics Research Journal* 3: 198–204.

Szinovacz, Maximiliane. 1987. "Family Power." In Beth Hess and Marvin Susman, eds. *The Sociology of Gender*, pp. 276–307. New York: Plenum Press.

Todd, Emmanuel. 1987. *Causes of Progress, Culture, Authority, and Change*. New York: Oxford University Press.

Ulrich, Laurel Thatcher. 1987. "Housewife and Goddess: Themes of Self-Sufficieny and Community in Eighteenth Century New England." In Carol Groneman and Mary Beth Norton, eds. *"To Toil the Livelong Day": America's Women at Work, 1780–1980*, pp. 21–34. Ithaca: Cornell University Press.

Waite, Linda. 1981. *U.S. Women at Work*. Population Bulletin no. 36 (May). Washington, D.C.: Population Reference Bureau.

Weber, Max. 1966. "Class, Status, and Party." In Reinhardt Bendix and Seymor M. Lipset, eds. *Class, Status, and Power*, pp. 21–28. New York: Free Press.

Welter, Barbara. 1978. "The Cult of True Womanhood: 1820–1860." In Michael Gordon, ed. *The American Family in Social-Historical Perspective*, pp. 313–333. 2d ed. New York: St. Martin's.

Williams, Norma. 1988. "Role-Making among Married Mexican-American Women: Issues of Class and Ethnicity." *Journal of Behavioral Science* 24: 75–89.

Whitney, Eleanor Noss, and Corrinne Baboy Cataldo. 1983. *Clinical Nutrition*. St. Paul, Minn.: West.

Wilson, Gail. 1987. *Money in the Family*. Brookfield, England: Gowen.

Wood, Mildred W., Ruth Linquist, and Lucy A. Studley. 1932. *Managing the Home*. Cambridge: Houghton Mifflin.

Woodward, Joanne. 1958. *Management and Technology*. London: Her Majesty's Stationery Office.

Yetley, Elizabeth A., Merwin J. Yetley, and Beningno Aguirri. 1978. "Family Role Structure and Food-Related Roles in Mexican-American Families." *Journal of Nutrition Education* 13 (supplement): 596–601.

Zey-Ferrell, Mary, ed. 1979. *Dimensions of Organizations: Environment, Context, Structure, Process and Performance*. Santa Monica, Calif.: Goodyear.

Zey-Ferrell, Mary, and Wm. Alex McIntosh. 1987. "Predicting and Understanding the Intent to Consume Beef among Texas Women." *Departmental Technical Report* no. 87-4. College Station: Department of Sociology, Texas A&M University.

WHAT DOES IT MEAN TO BE FAT, THIN, AND FEMALE IN THE UNITED STATES: A REVIEW ESSAY

Carole M. Counihan

Boskind-White, Marlene, and William C. White (1983). *Bulimarexia: The Binge/Purge Cycle.* New York: Norton.

Bruch, Hilde (1978). *The Golden Cage: The Enigma of Anorexia Nervosa.* New York: Vintage.

Chernin, Kim (1981). *The Obsession: Reflections on the Tyranny of Slenderness.* New York: Harper & Row.

Millman, Marcia (1980). *Such a Pretty Face: Being Fat in America.* New York: Norton.

Orbach, Susie (1978). *Fat Is a Feminist Issue: The Anti-Diet Guide to Permanent Weight Loss.* New York: Paddington.

The five books under review address what it means for women to be fat and thin in contemporary North America. They discuss in its extreme forms women's obsession with food: the compulsive eating of obesity, the self-starvation of anorexia nervosa, and the oscillating binging and purging of bulimarexia. All of these books are about women and, with the exception of one coauthor, all are by women. They are all feminist in that they link women's obsession with eating to broader social, political, and economic forces affecting women in 20th-century North America. They concur that the problematical relationship between women and food is invariably linked to women's difficulty in being women—to their feelings of powerlessness and sexual ambivalence—although they stress different forces in accounting for that difficulty. Forces they propose include the contradictory expectations of families for girls; the objectification of women and degradation of their sexuality; the institutionalized cultural, political, and economic powerlessness of women; and the cultural slighting of female experience and female values. An excessive concern with food is a product of and response to these important factors in American women's lives.

THE BOOKS

All five volumes provide social-psychological analyses of women's obsession with fat. They are compellingly and vibrantly written, and one reads them with fascination and ease. The authors present their insights in a clear and organized manner and support them with extensive quotations from female subjects. There emerges a humanistic sensitivity to women tormented by constant thoughts of food, tortured by starvation or gorging, caught in a vicious cycle of guilt, self-loathing, and despair. At the same time, the books are convincing; their data and arguments speak strongly.

Chernin's book ranges the most broadly of the five. Her insights come from her own vanquished food fixation; from observations of contemporary fashion and advertising; and from Western philosophy, literature, mythology, and psychology. She argues that the "tyranny of slenderness" is a product of the mind/body dichotomy fundamental to Western culture in which men hold power and are identified with the exalted mind, and women serve them and are likened to the denigrated body. Her feminism is as strong as her exuberant imagination in arguing that women's obsession with fat is "an effort to control or eliminate the passionate aspects of the self in order to gain the approval and prerogatives of masculine culture" and that this effort explains "all those particular sensations of emptiness, of longing and craving, of dread and despair" (p. 187) shared by compulsive eaters and starving anorexics.

While Chernin discusses both fat and thin, Millman and Orbach deal principally with overweight women, though all six authors view obesity and skeletal anorexia as two versions of the same obsession. Millman is a sociologist. Her data come principally from interviews with fat women and from participant observation at helping organizations for fat people: the National Association to Aid Fat Americans, Overeaters Anonymous, and a summer Diet Camp for children. Her book is richly sprinkled with her informants' words, which give pungency to the argument that fat is a sadly misdirected personal response to the grievous difficulty of being a woman in our society.

Orbach and the Whites are therapists. Their approaches are similar although Orbach deals with overeaters and the Whites with bulimarexics, compulsive eaters who gorge and then purge by self-induced vomiting, laxatives, diuretics, and violent exercise. Both use group therapy and attempt to help their patients deal with the problems of womanhood by building a positive female identity. Orbach takes a strongly feminist approach. She bases her inquiry and therapy on the question: "What is it about the social position of women that leads them to respond to it by getting fat?" (p. 19). The Whites take a similar approach to binging and purging. They contest traditional explanations of the obsession which blame it on the mother; Orbach goes further by showing how the paradoxical position of a socially oppressed mother raising a daughter into inevitable oppression is in part responsible for the problematical character of femininity and the mother–daughter relationship, which sometimes leads to eating disorders. Both books abound in observations of and by patients, and both contain concrete suggestions about specific group-therapy techniques that have been successful in aiding women overcome their obsession.

Hilde Bruch (1973, 1978) is a physician and psychotherapist who has been working with eating disorders for forty years. *The Golden Cage* is a moving discussion of anorexia nervosa based on close reference to the troubled girls Bruch has treated. Anorexia nervosa is the voluntary starvation that most often afflicts adolescent females from privileged backgrounds; like bulimarexia, it seems to have been increasing at an alarming rate in the last 15 to 20 years (Bruch 1978: viii). Bruch is the least overtly feminist of the authors under review, yet her findings contain an implicit indictment of U.S. society. Her patients are characterized by an undeveloped sense of self, overcompliance, and a fixation with being thin as the sole way to exert control over the world around them. Bruch locates the cause of this pathetic condition not in the victim but in forces around her, principally in familial and cultural expectations that women be unreasonably compliant and thin.

These books are not diet books, though all aim to help women achieve a more tranquil relationship to their bodies which may result in weight loss (see also Boskind-Lodahl 1976 and Orbach 1982). Nor are these books biophysiological investigations of food disorders; discussion of the hormonal and metabolic conditions of weight are in fact conspicuously lacking (see Bierman and Hirsch 1981 and Hirsch 1984. See also Beller 1977; Contento 1980; and Dyrenforth, Wooley and Wooley 1980, who specifically discuss female physiology, food, and fat). Although all the books refer to aspects of the social, political, and economic context in explaining the meaning of fat and thin, they do not explicitly consider political economy: the ways in which the evolution of North American capitalism has produced this particular form of mental slavery (see Aronson 1980;

Hacker 1980; Leghorn and Roodkowsky 1977). Finally, though relying heavily on informants' words, these books are not directly biographical (see Broughton 1978; Liu 1979; Roth 1982).

All five books take issue with traditional interpretations in several ways. First, they take eating disorders seriously, something that many physicians and psychologists fail to do (Broughton 1978; Chernin 1981: 1). The authors all understand how the simple command to diet or to eat, characteristic of many treatments, fails to address the underlying cause: identity confusion. Bruch (p. 107) specifically cautions against behavior modification therapy, which merely reinforces the sense of helplessness basic to the anorexics' problem; Millman (pp. 89–90) points out the futility of standard diet strategies, which have an estimated 90–95 percent recidivism rate (Beller 1977: 264). In their compassion for their subjects, the authors emphasize not the dangers of obesity—exaggerated by the media, medical plans, doctors, and insurance companies (Millman 1980: 87–88)—but the physiological burdens of constant weight fluctuations, fasting, and amphetamine consumption (see Broughton 1978), the stressful nervous effects of maintaining an excessively low body weight, and the isolating self-centeredness of the obsession. The Whites contest the regnant explanation of bulimarexia as a symptom of rejection of the traditional female role and posit that on the contrary it seems to be a consequence of an excessive adherence to that role. Ambivalence about that role is recognized by all the authors as part of the obsession. Orbach (1978: 17) rejects the Freudian diagnosis of obesity as "an obsessive-compulsive symptom related to separation-individuation, narcissism and insufficient ego-development." Her objections characterize the approach of the five books. They reject explanations of eating disorders as individual character failures. Disorders, rather, express conflicts in the social process of becoming an American woman.

CHARACTERISTICS OF THE OBSESSION

Four principal themes emerge from the books as explanations of eating disorders: confusion over sexual identity and sexuality; struggle with issues of power, control, and release; solitude and deceit; and family strife. Before examining these themes in detail, however, it is important to note differences among the three disorders. Obesity involves overeating to an extreme statistically determined as being from 10 to 25 percent over "normal" body weight. An estimated 40 percent of American women may be obese (Beller 1977: 6–9) and many more women "feel fat" (see Dyrenforth, Wolley and Wooley 1980). Fat people belong to all walks of life though there are proportionately more among the poor than among the rich (Millman 1980: 89). They are victims of vehement and irrational disgust, denigration, and discrimination (Millman 1980: 90; Beller 1977: 9; Dyrenforth, Wooley and Wooley 1980). Anorexia nervosa is voluntary starvation; as Bruch emphasizes, the physiological effects of starvation are crucial to the distorted perceptions of self and reality that make anorexia hard to treat. Anorexics tend to be white, adolescent girls from socially and economically advantaged families (Bruch 1978, chap. 2). The same is true for bulimarexics, but they include older women of more varied backgrounds as well (Boskind-White and White 1983, chap. 3). They tend to be thin but not starving and may go through long periods of eating normally before erupting into a cycle of binging and purging. Chronic bulimarexics may go through the cycle from once a week to as many as eighteen times per day, consuming from 1,000 to 20,000 calories per binge (Boskind-White and White 1983: 45). The Whites (p. 34) feel that bulimarexics are "more tenacious," more independent, and less needy of "showing" their pain than anorexics are. Yet the female subjects of these books, whether obese, starving, or compulsively gorging and vomiting, share an extreme obsession with food, an obsession, the authors suggest, whose characteristics strike a chord in all women.

1. Sexuality and Sexual Identity

"It is often this critical question of how women can define and manage their own sexuality that is being grappled with in the fat/thin dilemma" (Orbach 1978: 73). Like bulimarexics, anorexics and the obese "typically loathe their bodies" (Boskind-White and White 1983: 115). This hatred of the body often comes with adolescence, when the slim, androgynous body begins to change. One anorexic said, "I have a deep fear of having a womanly body, round and fully developed" (Bruch 1978: 85). Such fear often accompanies antipathy to menstruation: "It's like a conviction for a crime I never committed. I vow to prove my innocence somehow and release myself from this punishment" (Liu 1979: 34). Later, when Liu drops to 95 pounds and her periods consequently stop, as they always do for anorexics (Bruch 1978: 65), she rejoices, "I don't suppose the reprieve will last forever, but for the moment it delights me. And the more weight I lose, the flatter I become. It's wonderful, like crawling back into the body of a child" (Liu 1979: 41). While anorexics retreat from female maturity by becoming childlike and asexual, overweight women accomplish the same end by becoming fat. They become sexually neuter by violating cultural standards of ideal femininity (Millman 1980, chap. 6; Orbach 1978: 60).

The women under scrutiny here not only hate their bodies and fear their womanly shapes but are obsessively concerned with their size and weight. The thin constantly weigh themselves and assess their shape in mirrors; the fat retreat from looking but cannot escape their thoughts. Their common concern involves establishing unrealistic standards for themselves and holding a distorted perception of their own and other bodies (Bruch 1978: 81): "thin is never thin enough" (Boskind-White and White 1983: 29).

Characteristic of women's troubled relationship to their bodies is a conscious opposition of mind and body which becomes a sense of being split in two (Boskind-White and White 1983: 33) or of being disembodied (Chernin 1981: 55; Millman 1980, chap. 9). Fat women refuse to look at or even acknowledge their bodies, so great is their loathing and shame for their expansiveness: "I feel so terrible about the way I look that I cut off connection with my body. I operate from the neck up. I do not look in mirrors" (Millman 1980: 195). Anorexics "speak of feeling divided, as being a split person or two people" and, significantly, "when they define this separate aspect, this different person seems always to be a male" (Bruch 1978: 58).

Dieting becomes an attempt to eliminate or render invisible that part of the self represented by the body (Orbach 1978: 169). A woman's attempt to escape hunger is "a terrible struggle against her sensual nature" (Chernin 1981: 10), a struggle destined to failure because all human beings have physiological needs that cannot be denied. According to Chernin, women's antipathy toward their own sensuality reflects Western culture's repression of appetite, which may be particularly strong within the Puritan tradition. The obese, anorexics, and bulimarexics all display an irrational terror of hunger which is often accompanied by an inability effectively to allow, recognize, or satisfy the physiological stirrings of appetite (Bruch 1978, p. 42–43; Orbach 1978: 108).They may also feel disgust and fear toward sexual contact (Bruch 1978: 73) and a great insecurity about their own sexuality. There may be an unsatisfied longing for sexual intimacy as well (Chernin 1981, chap. 4; Millman 1980, chap. 6; Orbach 1978: 60). "Sexuality is a great wasteland of unfulfilled pleasures, confusion, guilt, fear, and disgust" (Boskind-White and White 1983: 113).

Obsession with food serves as an escape: "It distracted me from problems like the future, my parents' marriage, men, and all the other questions over which I had absolutely no control" (Liu 1979: 109). Obesity serves as a buffer between a woman and men. Being fat makes her unattractive, asexual, and remote, and she can avoid sex entirely (Millman 1980: 172). Though being excessively thin begins as an attempt to satisfy the cultural ideal of "slim is beautiful," it also isolates women from sexual encounters. The excessive pursuit of weight loss results in androgyny:

a boyish body without breasts or menstruation, the overt and insistent symbols of femininity (Bruch 1978: 64–65; Orbach 1978: 169). Liu (1979: 87) says, "Maybe, I mused, if I lost enough weight, men would start to ignore me. Sometimes I felt it would be worth it to bind my breasts and veil my face."

These five books address the question as to why women have such a troubled relationship to sexuality. After all, sexual pleasure can be wonderful, and women's sexuality is linked to their generative power. Yet, the books suggest, in North America female sexuality is not venerated but rather is degraded and objectified. In fashion and the media women are repeatedly presented with idealized images of themselves. Pornography—degrading sexual violence—is directed at women with the most splendidly voluptuous female bodies (Chernin 1981: 133), while men idealize as beautiful a standard of thinness that for most adult women is inaccessible. An attractive woman with a normally curvacious body is subject to leers, whistles, come-ons, and vulgar comments from men. She may feel assessed first as a physical object, only second as a human subject (Liu 1979). Some women attempt to flee from the objectification and degradation of their sexuality by becoming asexual through excessive thinness or fatness.

Chernin is the only author to propose an overt explanation for the denigration of female sexuality and plumpness in our society. She links it to the mind/body split basic to Western ideology which "may well characterize patriarchal culture altogether" (p. 56). The body and its passions are set apart from the mind and identified with oppressed groups—women and also Blacks (p. 129). Men's power over these groups is an assertion of their control over those passionate, sensual, instinctual, and explosive tendencies that represent all in life that is threatening. In addition, Chernin suggests, men fear and envy women's sexuality and fertility. They cope with their own feelings of sexual inadequacy and jealousy of women's procreative ability by devaluing sex and procreation. This devaluation serves as an ideological buffer to male power—a power that is wielded in the economy, in politics, and in culture. In women's problematical relationship to food we also see their struggle to deal with their lack of power.

2. Power, Control, and Release

The books share the perspective of popular feminism that the denigration of women's physicality parallels the cultural subordination of their values and ways of being, which extends even to the muting of their voices (Gilligan 1983). "Men both act for them and describe their experience" (Orback 1978: 71). The books suggest that the growth of the feminist movement and rise in working women have increased the contradictions of the female role. Women have not surrendered their traditional expectations of being wives and mothers, but they have added new goals of productive work and independent public identity (Howe 1977). They are educated to be passive and compliant but find these postures unsuited to success in the workplace. They want to be producers but find society casting them in the role of consumers and loading that role with more conflicts: eat junk foods but don't get fat; wear sexy clothes but be a faithful wife. The tensions in living out these conflicts, according to the five books, can become unbearable, especially for women lacking a strong sense of self. Some respond through compulsively restricted or excessive eating.

Anorexics and bulimarexics are particularly notable for their over-compliance. The former are typical "good girls" who have always done what they were supposed to do (Bruch 1978, chap. 3; Liu 1979: 39). Bulimarexics are typically extremely subservient to men (Boskind-White and White 1983: 20). Anorexic, bulimarexic, and overweight women all have a difficult time asserting themselves, going against societal or familial programs, and choosing their own paths. Food becomes the one sure way they can exert control in the world: "When the rest of my life is going out of control I always say to myself, there's one thing I *can* control, what I put in my mouth" (Millman 1980: 161). Some women exercise this control by eating and becoming fat. Physical bulk can be a source of power, giving women stature and removing them from the category of frail, helpless females (Orbach 1978, chap. 2). For many women, however, control consists of denying themselves food. The anorexic "Betty explained that losing weight was giving her power, that each pound lost was like a treasure that added to her power" (Bruch 1978: 5). Starving becomes a channel to achievement: "In this one respect, I'm the best, but if I let it go, all is lost, and so I cling to my diet tenaciously" (Liu 1979: 40).

But while food may be a domain for control, it can be a channel for losing control, for attaining release and repose:

> The inside of a binge is deep and dark; it is a descent into a world in which every restriction you have placed on yourself is cut loose. The forbidden is obtainable. Nothing matters—not friends, not family, not lovers. Nothing matters but food. Lifting, chewing, swallowing—mechanical frenzied acts, one following the other until a physical limit, usually nausea, is reached. Then comes the sought after numbness, the daze, the indifference to emotional pain. Like a good drug, food knocks out sensation (Roth 1982: 15–16).

Compulsive eaters describe over and over again the oblivion and ecstasy they achieve while binging. "Some people describe binging not only as taking place outside of rational consciousness, but like getting drunk, as being an activity that actually *produces* a state of unconsciousness" (Millman, 1980: 141). One girl described anorexia as "It is as if you were slowly poisoned, something like being under the chronic influence of something like alcohol or dope" (Bruch 1978: 15). Eating can also be a substitute for sexual release and a way of trying to fill emotional hunger (Chernin 1981: 11). "I'm taking care of everyone else, and food takes care of me" (Millman 1980: 109).

Furthermore, the six authors point out, women are trained to be non-aggressive, pacifying, and self-sacrificing. They are conditioned not to express strong emotions (Orbach 1978: 52). So if they feel angry about job discrimination or their husbands' failure to help around the house, they may react by turning their anger against themselves: eating eating eating, or starving starving starving. The food fixation blots out other battles. Many women, in fact, put off living fully until after they have resolved their struggle with food. Characteristic of all women obsessed with food is this postponement, accompanied by a transformation fantasy: "Once I am thin, everything will change ... " (see Atwood 1976: 47; Boskind-White and White 1983: 158; Millman 1980, chap. 10; Orbach 1978: 132–33). Women are socialized to believe that their problems come from being too fat. Being thin then becomes a panacea, a totally absorbing quest, a pathetically reductionist channel for attaining control in a world where they suffer institutionalized powerlessness.

3. Solitude, Withdrawal, Deceit, Competition

One of the strongest characteristics of the food obsession that emerges in the five books is its individualism. Women gorge, purge, or starve in secret. Their attitudes toward their obsession—whether the pride of the anorexic or the guilt of the compulsive eater—serve to isolate them further. Like anorexics, all these women become "completely self-absorbed.... Food thoughts crowd out their ability to think about anything else" (Bruch 1978: 79). They practice their rituals—of gorging, vomiting, scrutinizing their bodies in the mirror, or fanatically exercising—alone. The need to hide their weird behavior from others and to lie about their eating habits leads to increasing withdrawal. Deceit becomes fundamental to their lifestyle and leads in turn to increasing self-hatred, despair, and withdrawal. The solitude of these tormented women can only exacerbate what the books suggest is one of the main underlying causes of their obsession: their poorly developed sense of self. One might ponder whether the social atomization characteristic of the United States facilitates the secrecy and increases the isolation of these women, further hindering exit from their compulsion.

Their solitude is often characterized by competition with and mistrust of others, particularly other women. Anorexics take pride in being superior to—that is, thinner than—other girls (Bruch 1978: 18). Liu is reluctant to tell her friends the secret of her extreme weight loss lest they weaken her triumph by becoming thinner than she. "Bulimarexic women are constantly comparing their bodies—and their lives in general—to those of other women—and almost always unfavorably, with further loss of self-esteem" (Boskind-White and White 1983: 38).

Orbach (1978: 49–51) explicitly argues that the difficulty women in the United States have in dealing with competition permeates their struggle with food, and data from the other books support her thesis. While men are socialized to achieve and trained in techniques of success, competition in women, particularly with men, is seen as unfeminine. Female socialization emphasizes cooperation; women who strive for competitive achievement may find themselves on foreign and threatening terrain (Gilligan 1983: 42; Orbach 1978: 49–51). Getting fat may be a way of coping with difficult feelings about competition—by hiding the feelings behind the wall of fat, by allowing women to use the body as an excuse for failure, and by providing in compulsive eating an outlet for uncomfortable competitive feelings (Orbach 1978: 51).

Again, however, the authors expose the futility of the struggle. In a society that institutionalizes competition in every aspect of life—for grades, for jobs, for shape—at the same time as it denies women the ability to compete and still be feminine, it is no wonder that women opt out of the competition, internalize it, or limit it to the trivial domain of body weight. Women's isolated, competitive individualism in their struggle with food, the books suggest, is an internalization of the competitive values and practices fundamental to U.S. society. The society tends to define all problems as individual ones and to suggest that they can be overcome by personal effort aimed at raising oneself above others. The result is to focus individual rage not against society but against the self, and it permits the continuance of a status quo built on the systematic oppression of women.

4. Family Strife

The five books contend that anorexia, bulimarexia, and obesity respond not only to the social conditions of womanhood but also to familial organization. Food is a central, readily available battleground for issues of "autonomy, control and love" (Millman 1980: 72) in the growing girl's relationship with her parents. Anorexics have a history of being "perfect" daughters, and their starvation is a way of expressing their feelings of powerlessness and their anger at their parents for depriving them of the right to live their own lives (Bruch 1978: 38). The heroine of Atwood's *Lady Oracle* (1976) stuffs herself like "a beluga whale" (p. 78) as a way of waging war against her mother and demanding autonomy. Refusal to eat is also an act of defiance (Bruch 1978: 38). Starvation may allow the anorexic to return to a childlike dependence on her parents to feed her and thus free her from the burden of their expectations. Triumphant self-denial may provide her with a concrete outlet for achievement in a world of privilege in which she feels inconsequential. Bruch's patient who described herself as "a sparrow in a golden cage" (p. 24) captures this feeling, and Liu's words describe the situation typical of many anorexics and bulimarexics: "Mine was a childhood frosted with affluence, filled with adventure, and sprinkled generously with loving care. Throughout the early years I led a cupcake existence, wrapped in my parents' unspoken promises that they had me destined for the best of all possible worlds (1979: 1).

These high expectations and privileged family conditions make all the more painful the girls' encounter with the difficulties of female achievement in "the real world." At home the girls encounter the different possibilities open to their brothers (Boskind-White and White 1983, chap. 4) and the lack of societal approval of their mothers' achievements. Indeed, these mothers are often women who gave up aspirations of careers to devote themselves to their families (Bruch 1978: 28). They may simultaneously be seething with resentment, living life again by pushing their daughters to go further than they did, proving by their own limits the difficulty of female achievement, and attempting to validate their own lives by limiting their daughters (Orbach 1978: 26–32). Daughters may be angry at mothers for their dominance and overinvolvement, for their subservience to their husbands, and for their failure to achieve (Boskind-White and White 1983: 67ff; Liu 1979). Daughters may be angry at their fathers for being cold, domineering, and distant (Boskind-White and White 1983: 172–74) or for being sexually threatening (Millman 1980: 173–74). Overeating and self-starvation are ways of asserting control, demanding attention, and expressing anger. They are ultimately self-destructive ways, however, which do nothing to alter the social conditions that produce distant and idealized father–daughter relations and conflict-ridden mother–daughter relations. As Orbach (1978: 113) says,

As long as patriarchal culture demands that women bring up their daughters to accept an inferior social position, the mother's job will be fraught with tension and confusion which are often made manifest in the way mothers and daughters interact over the subject of food.

5. Why Now?

Reported cases of anorexia and bulimarexia have increased alarmingly in the last 15 to 20 years (Bruch 1978: viii), and concern with obesity also appears to be rising (Chernin 1981, chap. 9). Several reasons are suggested by the five books under review.

First, the affluence of white, middle-class North America makes food plentiful. In the context of abundance, voluntary starvation is a powerful symbolic act (Bruch 1978: 9; Chernin 1981: 103). But societal affluence also means that women can allow themselves the luxury of overeating or of binging and vomiting a week's worth of groceries in a day (Boskind-White and White 1983: 48). The growing prevalence of junk foods means women can overeat yet never satisfy the body's craving for adequate nutrition. As John Keats (1976: 12) said, "Some Americans are now starving to death even as they gain weight."

The U.S. food industry contributes to the problem (see Aronson 1980; Hacker 1980; Hess and Hess 1977; Hightower 1975). Like all capitalist endeavors, it must grow to remain viable. With a relatively stable population, advertising must create markets for new foods. Once women have converted these foods into fat, they are exhorted to buy diet foods to shed the fat. The economy depends on manipulating consumers to buy as much as possible, and one way is to project simultaneously the urge to eat and the need to diet.

Current standards of fashion and beauty contribute to women's obsession with food by projecting a particularly thin ideal. Chernin notes that standards for female beauty have fluctuated over the years in the United States and have demanded the greatest thinness at times when women have demanded greatest rights. She points out that as feminism's projection of strong women has increased, so have child pornography and incest (pp. 108–9), and she ventures: "In this age of feminist assertion, men are drawn to women of childish body and mind because there is something less disturbing about the vulnerability and helplessness of a small child—and something truly disturbing about the body and mind of a mature woman" (p. 110). The media contribute by promoting a thin ideal that is almost impossible to attain and whose attainment will result in the literal physical weakness of undernourishment for most women (see Kaufman 1980). This ideal increases the distance between a woman and herself, exacerbating her conflicts and making it harder for her to be at one with herself—hence the obsession.

Feminism has also raised women's expectations about their potential lives. But real opportunities have not kept pace, increasing the disparity between hopes and reality (Bruch 1978: ix; Chernin 1981, chap. 9). Furthermore, feminism has demanded an end to all double standards, including sexual ones. In conjunction with the loosening of sex mores which has permeated our entire culture, this demand has led to increasing pressure on girls to have sexual relations ever earlier. "Greater sexual freedom may be a factor in the greater frequency of anorexia nervosa" (Bruch 1978: ix) and in bulimarexia (Boskind-White and White 1983: 90), by augmenting the adolescent's anxiety about her transition to womanhood.

ALTERNATIVES TO THE OBSESSION

We have noted the common characteristics of obesity, anorexia nervosa, and bulimarexia, and the cultural problems of womanhood to which they respond. The five books under review point out that the responses are self-destructive and unproductive, and offer alternatives.

Being excessively fat or thin does challenge stereotypes of femininity through their negation but leaves victims with only negation. Such responses offer neither a new positive self-image nor all empowering analysis of why our society's female stereotype is damaging and oppressive (Millman 1980, chap. 5). They do not attack what Bruch implies and the other authors state is the basis of the obsession: the subordinate position of women in society. Bulimarexia, anorexia, and obesity all catch their victims in a vicious cycle of guilt and despair. The women punish themselves over and over again; they eat, starve, or binge and purge to escape their shame and desperation; they end up hating themselves more than before; and again they plunge into their excesses, to forget or punish themselves further. In the process they ruin their health, weaken their bodies, and render themselves socially ineffectual as obese nonpersons or as "invisible" anorexics (Orbach 1978: 146). All their energies are focused on food; all their hope is pinned on the expected miracle of transformation that will occur when they defeat their obsession.

All five books propose an alternative to eating or starving. The alternative is based essentially on developing a strong, positive sense of female identity. It involves teaching women to make their personal problems part of a broader social analysis. Here the books prescribe techniques common to popular feminist pedagogy: intellectual liberation through discussion of oppression, and self-help and support groups. With anorexics, Bruch insists that the first step is to counter the severe psychophysiological effects of starvation by raising body weight, through hospitalization if necessary. Then therapy should aim at penetrating the web of dishonesty, self-deception, and overcompliance characteristic of anorexics, to develop "a valid self-concept and the capacity for self-directed action" (1978: 130). Orbach and the Whites suggest that their patients cease tormenting themselves about *why* they eat compulsively and ask what their behavior *does* for them, so that they can come up with other ways of doing the same things and reduce their total reliance on food as panacea. Food obsession is not the entire problem but the channel through which deeper psychosocial problems are worked out. Hence they propose healing strategies that focus on uncovering and dealing with the problems below the surface.

All of the authors believe in the benefits for women of recognizing that others share the obsession. The Whites and Orbach practice group therapy, which aims to help women out of their loneliness, make their problem less shameful and easier to bear, provide perspective, and strengthen their weak self-image. It also teaches women to be assertive, to use their mouths to express anger rather than to eat (Orbach 1978: 58). All the authors imply that women need to learn that contrary to what society tells them, their identity consists of more than how they look. The books share one important principle of contemporary popular feminism in their common recognition that the possibility of autonomous action is the first essential step to vanquishing the food fixation.

FURTHER QUESTIONS

Several questions come to mind as one ponders the data and explanations these books offer about excessively fat and thin women. If these excesses are responses to the problematical character of being a woman, why do men also suffer from eating disorders? About one-tenth of Bruch's anorexic patients are male (1978: viii), and "seriously overweight" men seem to be nearly as common as women (Beller 1977: 6). There are no figures on bulimarexic men; they seem to be few or nonexistent, though they may just be sociologically invisible. Of the five books, only Millman's explicitly considers male eating disorders, in an appendix entitled "Fat Men, a Different Story." Because her interviews with men involved a smaller, older, and more restricted group than her female sample, she is cautious, but she finds that the male experience of being fat is vastly different from the female. Men think less about being fat; they are less prone to connect it with psychological, personal, or emotional problems; they fight social disdain rather than internalizing it; and they really do not think obesity affects their relationships, careers, or masculinity. In short, they live relatively easily with their fat. Gay men, however, seem to be as concerned about weight as women are. Millman (1980: 244) suggests, "As we are all increasingly socialized to be consumers rather than producers, men as well as women will be evaluated increasingly in terms of how they measure up to media images of attractiveness rather than their achievements in work. Thus men's experiences with weight will increasingly resemble those of women." Perhaps men who suffer from eating disorders have found themselves through particular familial and social situations in positions of extreme powerlessness, overcompliance, and poor self-image. If societal conditions through concentrating economic and political power produce more dependent and insecure men, there may well be an increase in men suffering from eating disorders.

If the food obsession is connected closely with a girl's troubled transition to womanhood, why do preadolescent children experience it as well? Cam Reed was a compulsive eater for as long as she can remember; her autobiography begins with recollections of ecstasy over the arrival of the ice-cream truck (Broughton 1978). The heroine of *Lady Oracle* (Atwood 1976: 43) recounts that in her earliest baby pictures, "I was never looking at the camera; instead I was trying to get something into my mouth." Some children, both boys and girls, appear to bave a tendency from the very beginning to eat a lot, and/or to gain weight easily (Beller 1977, chap. 2).

There are biological forces that affect desires for food, weight gain, and the ability normally to recognize and satisfy hunger. None of our five books considers them, but Beller's (1977) does at length and suggests that biology and evolution have played a great role in both shaping a given individual's relation to food and in facilitating weight gain in women. Although social and psychological factors may be extremely important in contributing to eating disorders, some people may become excessively fat because of how their bodies work. Biological, genetic, and endocrinological studies can make important contributions to this question, and failure to consider them weakens the books under review.

If very young children exhibit noticeably different yearnings for food, one wonders not only about the influence of individual and sexual biology but also about the role of feeding patterns in early infancy. Orbach (1978: 30) cites a study that showed significant differences in how mothers breastfed daughters and sons. Crosscultural data (Du Bois 1941, 1960; Mead 1935; D. Shack 1969; W. Shack 1971) suggest that feeding practices can have a lifelong effect on a child's personality and relationship to food. More studies are needed to determine to what extent early childhood feeding in the United States is responsible for the obsession with food and its particular form.

Are there women who are fat and happy in the United States? The books describe a host of overweight women who are misersble. The authors imply that a successful struggle with the social and psychological constraints on becoming female will result in tranquility with self and usually a loss of weight. But are there women at ease with themselves and their social positions who are fat because they eat a lot and with pleasure? There are fat women in other cultures, in Italy for example (Counihan 1983), who accept weight gain as part of the inevitable and normal process of maturation. Fat Samoan women seem to be content with their size and, significantly, suffer none of the hypertention associated with obesity in the United States (MacKenzie in Chernin 1981: 32). Is a certain amount of fat biologically "normal"? But is our society so full of conflicts as to render a happy, healthy, sociable fat woman an impossibility?

Crosscultural comparisons can offer insights. First of all, they show that in many other societies (Beller 1977, chap. 1) and even in different historical periods (Beller 1977, Chernin 1981) and subcultures (Styles 1980) within our own society, weight in women is socially acceptable. W. Shack (1971) discovered among the Gurage of Ethiopia that *men* suffer an eating obsession involving spirit possession and gorging to satisfy and purge the evil spirit. DeGarine and Koppert (1984) describe the *guru* ritual of the Massa of the Cameroons, which involves seclusion and fattening of young men who then gain enormous social prestige and attractiveness. Further crosscultural investigations can test the feminist explanation for the food obsession in the United States by investigating the relationship between the societal valuation of women, their autonomy, their attitudes toward their bodies, and their body sizes. In particular, data from societies without the political and economic stratification that characterizes our own can offer perspective on how women's obsession with food is a product of their powerlessness in the United States.

NOTE

I thank Roger Haydon, Steve Kaplan, Theresa Rubin, Jolane Solomon, and anonymous reviewers for comments on earlier drafts of this paper.

REFERENCES

Aronson, Naomi (1980). "Working up an Appetite." In Kaplan 1980, pp. 201–31.
Atwood, Margaret (1976). *Lady Oracle*. New York: Avon.

Beller, Anne Scott (1977). *Fat and Thin: A Natural History of Obesity.* New York: Farrar, Straus & Giroux.

Bierman, Edwin L., and Jules Hirsch (1981). "Obesity." In *Textbook of Endocrinology*, ed. by Robert H. Williams. Philadelphia: Saunders, pp. 907–21.

Boskind-Lodahl, Marlene (1976). "Cinderella's Stepsisters: A Feminist Perspective on Anorexia Nervosa and Bulimarexia." *Signs* 2: 342–56.

Boskind-White, Marlene, and William C. White (1983). *Bulimarexia. The Binge/Purge Cycle.* New York: Norton.

Broughton, Diane (1978). *Confessions of a Compulsive Eater.* Nashville: Nelson.

Bruch, Hilde (1973). *Eating Disorders: Obesity, Anorexia Nervosa and the Person Within.* New York: Basic.

Bruch, Hilde (1978). *The Golden Cage: The Engima of Anorexia Nervosa.* New York: Vintage.

Chernin, Kim (1981). *The Obsession: Reflections on the Tyranny of Slenderness.* New York: Harper & Row.

Contento, Isobel (1980). "The Nutritional Needs of Women." In Kaplan (1980), pp. 178–99.

Counihan, Carole M. (1983). "The Food Lives of Florentine Women: Nurturing Dependence." Unpublished manuscript.

DeGarine, Igor, and G. Koppert (1984). "Fatness and Culture Among the Massa (Cameroons): The Guru Institution." Unpublished manuscript.

DuBois, Cora (1941). "Attitudes toward Food and Hunger in Alor." In *Language, Culture and Personality: Essays in Memory of Edward Sapir.* eds. by Leslie Spier, A. Irving Hallowell, and Stanley S. Newman. Monasha, Wise.: Sapir Memorial Publication Fund, pp. 272–81.

DuBois, Cora (1960). *The People of Alor.* Cambridge: Harvard University Press.

Dyrenforth, Sue R., Orland W. Wooley, and Susan C. Wooley (1980). "A Woman's Body in a Man's World: A Review of Findings on Body Image and Weight Control." In Kaplan 1980, pp. 29–57.

Gilligan, Carol (1982). *In a Different Voice: Psychological Theory and Women's Development.* Cambridge: Harvard University Press.

Hacker, Sally (1980). "Farming out the Home: Women and Agribusiness." In Kaplan 1980, pp. 235–63.

Hess, John L., and Karen Hess (1977). *The Tanse of America.* New York: Penguin.

Hightower, Jim (1975). *Eat your Heart Out: Food Profiteering in America.* New York: Crown.

Hirsch, Jules (1984). Hypothalamic Control of Appetite. *Hospital Practice.* February, pp. 131–38.

Howe, Louise Kapp (1977). *Pink Collar Workers: Inside the World of Women's Work.* New York: Avon.

Kaplan, Jane Rachel, ed. (1980). *A Woman's Conflict: The Special Relationship between Women and Food.* Englewood Cliffs, N. J.: Prentice-Hall.

Kaufman, Lois (1980). "Prime-Time Nutrition." *Journal of Communication.* Summer, pp. 37–46.

Keats, John (1976). *What Ever Happened to Mom's Apple Pie?* Boston: Houghton Mifflin.

Leghorn, Lisa, and Mary Roodkowsky (1977). *Who Really Starves? Women and World Hunger.* New York: Friendship.

Liu, Aimee (1979). *Solitaire.* New York: Harper & Row.

Mead, Margaret (1935). *Sex and Temperament in Three Primitive Societies.* New York: Morrow.

Millman, Marcia (1980). *Such a Pretty Face: Being Fat in America.* New York: Norton.

Orbach, Susie (1978). *Fat is a Feminist Issue: The Anti-Diet Guide to Permanent Weight Loss.* New York: Paddington.

Orbach, Susie (1982). *Fat is a Feminist Issue, II: A Program to Conquer Compulsive Eating.* New York: Berkeley.

Roth, Geneen (1982). *Feeding the Hungry Heart: The Experience of compulsive Eating.* New York: Signet.

Shack, Dorothy N. (1969). "Nutritional Processes and Personality Development among the Gurage." *Ethnology* 8: 292–300.

Shack, William A. (1971). "Hunger, Anxiety and Ritual: Deprivation and Spirit Possession among the Gurage of Ethiopia." *Man* 6, 1: 30–43.

Styles, Marvalene H. (1980). "Soul, Black Women and Food." In Kaplan (1980), pp. 161–76.

INDEX

ABOUT THE CONTRIBUTORS

Carole M. Counihan is associate professor of anthropology at Millersville University of Pennsylvania. She, along with Penny Van Esterik, is co-editor of *Food and Culture: A Reader* (Routledge 1997), and has published several articles on food, the body, gender and power based on her fieldwork in Florence, Sardinia, and the United States. Currently, Counihan is researching gender and food in the Southwest. She received her PhD from the University of Massachusetts, Amherst.

Miriam Kahn is assistant professor of anthropology at the University of Washington, Seattle. She is the author of *Always Hungry, Never Greedy: Food and the Expression of Gender in a Melanesian Society* (CUP 1986; Waveland 1994), which analyzes food symbolism and agricultural development. She is also the curator of Asian and Pacific ethnology at the Burke Museum of Natural History and Culture at the University of Washington. Recently, Kahn began research in French Polynesia on images of place, tourism, and nuclear testing. Kahn received her PhD from Bryn Mawr College.

Steven Laurence Kaplan is Goldwin Smith Professor of European History at Cornell University. Founder and editor of the journal *Food and Foodways*, Kaplan is also author of *The Bakers of Paris and the Bread Question, 1700–1775* (Duke University Press 1996), and *Farewell Revolution: The Historians' Feud, France, 1789/1989* (Cornell University Press 1995). He was appointed Chevalier de l'Ordre des Arts e des Lettres by the French government in 1996. Kaplan received his PhD from Yale University.

Kathryn S. March is associate professor of anthropology and women's studies at Cornell University. She is the co-author of *Mutual Regards: America and Nepal Seen Through Each Other's Eyes* (Jeevan Support Press 1994) and *Women's Informal Associations in Developing Countries: Catalysts for Change?* (Westview 1985). Currently, March's research focuses upon the enthnohistorical construction of Tamang gender, as well as the representation of Tamang identity and ritual practice. She received her PhD from Cornell University.

Wm. Alex McIntosh is professor of sociology at Texas A&M University. He is the author of *Sociologies of Food and Nutrition* (Plenum 1996). Recently, his articles have appeared in *Appetite, Journal of Applied Social Science, Journal of the American Dietetic Association,* and *Wellness Perspectives.* McIntosh has also contributed chapters to two forthcoming edited works: *The Social Appetite* (Oxford University Press), and *Food and Global History* (Westview). He received his PhD from Iowa State University.

Donald K. Pollock is an independent scholar in Washington, D.C. who has taught anthropology at Boston University, Harvard Medical School, and the State University of New York at Buffalo. His study of Kulina ethnomedicine, *Violent Delights: Kulina Ethnomedicine,* will soon be published by Cambridge University Press. He received his PhD from the University of Rochester.

Penny Van Esterik is professor of anthropology at York University, Toronto. Her recent books include *Beyond the Breast-Bottle Controversy* (Rutgers University Press 1989) and *Taking Refuge: Lao Buddhists in North America* (York Lanes 1993). Van Esterik, along with Carole Counihan, is co-editor of *Food and Culture: A Reader* (Routledge 1997). She is currently completing a book on gender in Thailand and plans to continue her research on breastfeeding and feminist theory. She received her PhD from the University of Illinois, Urbana.

Mary Zey is professor of sociology at Texas A&M University, specializing in economic sociology, complex organizations and theory. She is author of *Rational Choice and Organizational Theory: A Critique* (Sage 1997), *Banking on Fraud* (de Gruyter 1993), and *Dimensions of Organizations* (Goodyear of Prentice Hall 1979). Zey is also the editor of *Decision Making: Alternatives to Rational Choice Models* (Sage 1992) and *Complex Organizations: Critical Perspectives* (Scott, Foresman 1981). She received her PhD from Louisiana State University.